Selection
of Barcelona Hotels
and Restaurants

In the following pages, we offer a sampling of recommended establishments in Barcelona. The list is by no means exhaustive, but is designed to provide a few pointers to help you when making your choice.

Hotels have been selected according to their facilities and location, and whether they offer something extra in the way of charm, picturesque setting or historic associations. The number of stars for each hotel is awarded under the Spanish grading system. We have divided the hotels into the following price ranges, based on the cost of a double room with bath or shower.

Higher-priced above ptas. 20,000
Medium-priced ptas. 10,000–20,000
Lower-priced up to ptas. 10,000

We cannot guarantee the accuracy of these prices, which should be used as an approximate guide only. Please note that during the Olympic fortnight (25 July–9 August 1992) hotel accommodation will be extremely hard to find and rates will probably be considerably higher than those shown here.

Our criteria for restaurants are quality of cuisine, ambiance and service. For each address we mention any special features, and regular closing days, if any. Most restaurants also have periods of annual closing, usually in August, at Christmas and Easter. Phoning ahead to check is always wise, as is advance reservation. We have grouped the restaurants also into three categories according to price. Prices reflect the cost of an à la carte three-course meal without drinks.

Higher-priced above ptas. 4,000
Medium-priced ptas. 3,000–4,000
Lower-priced up to ptas. 3,000

HOTELS

HIGHER-PRICED
(above ptas. 20,000)

Alexandra ★★★★
Mallorca 251
08008 **Barcelona**
Tel. 215 30 52; tlx. 81107;
fax 216 06 06
75 rooms.

Avenida Palace ★★★★★
Gran Via de les Corts Catalanes
605

08007 **Barcelona**
Tel. 301 96 00; tlx. 54734;
fax 318 12 34
211 rooms. Deluxe hotel.
Excellent, attentive service.

Diplomatic ★★★★★
Pau Claris 122
08009 **Barcelona**
Tel. 317 31 00; tlx. 54701;
fax 318 65 31
215 rooms. Swimming pool.

Gran Derby ★★★★
Loreto 28
08029 **Barcelona**
Tel. 322 32 15; tlx. 97429;
fax 410 08 62
38 rooms. Exceptionally pleasant.

Gran Hotel Calderón ★★★★
Rambla de Catalunya 26
08007 **Barcelona**
Tel. 301 00 00; tlx. 51549;
fax 317 31 57
*244 rooms. Indoor and outdoor
swimming pools.*

Hilton ★★★★★
Avda. Diagonal 589–591
08014 **Barcelona**
Tel. 419 22 33; tlx. 99623;
fax 322 52 91
290 rooms. Modern hotel.

Majéstic ★★★★
Passeig de Gràcia 70
08005 **Barcelona**
Tel. 215 45 12; tlx. 52211;
fax 215 77 73
*344 rooms. Picturesque, central
location. Swimming pool, terrace.*

Melià Barcelona Sarrià ★★★★★
Avda. de Sarrià 50
08029 **Barcelona**
Tel. 410 60 60; tlx. 51638;
fax 321 51 79
*314 rooms. Modern hotel.
Picturesque setting in Sarrià.*

Presidente ★★★★★
Avda. Diagonal 570
08021 **Barcelona**
Tel. 200 21 11; tlx. 52180;
fax 209 51 06
*161 rooms. Modern hotel with
luxury facilities. Swimming pool.*

Princesa Sofía ★★★★★
Plaça Pius XII s/n
08028 **Barcelona**
Tel. 330 71 11; tlx. 51032;
fax 330 76 21
*505 rooms. Luxury hotel.
Picturesque setting, terrace.
Swimming pool.*

Ramada Renaissance ★★★★★
Rambla 111
08002 **Barcelona**
Tel. 318 62 00; tlx. 54634;
fax 301 77 76
210 rooms. Central location.

Ritz ★★★★★
Gran Via de les Corts Catalanes
668
08010 **Barcelona**
Tel. 318 52 00; tlx. 52739;
fax 318 01 48
*197 rooms. Most elegant of
luxury hotels.*

MEDIUM-PRICED
(ptas. 10,000–20,000)

Aragón ★★★
Aragó 569 bis
08026 **Barcelona**
Tel. 245 89 05; tlx. 98718;
fax 447 09 23
78 rooms.

Arenas ★★★★
Capità Arenas 20
08034 **Barcelona**
Tel. 204 03 00; tlx. 54990;
fax 205 65 06
59 rooms.

Barcelona ★★★★
Casp 1–13
08010 **Barcelona**
Tel. 302 58 58; tlx. 54990
67 rooms. Central location.

Colón ★★★★
Avda. Catedral 7
08002 **Barcelona**
Tel. 301 14 04; tlx. 52654;
fax 317 29 15
161 rooms.

Comtes de Barcelona ★★★★
Passeig de Gràcia 75
08008 **Barcelona**
Tel. 215 06 16; tlx. 51531;
fax 216 08 35
*100 rooms. Modern, centrally
located hotel in beautiful setting.
Impeccable facilities and service.*

Cristal ★★★★
Diputació 257
08011 **Barcelona**
Tel. 301 66 00; tlx. 54560
148 rooms.

Gótico ★★★
Jaume I 14
08002 **Barcelona**
Tel. 315 22 11; tlx. 97206;
fax 315 38 19
*72 rooms. Picturesque, central
location.*

Gran Hotel Cristina ★★★★
Avda. Diagonal 458
08036 **Barcelona**
Tel. 217 68 00; tlx. 54328;
fax 217 69 00
123 rooms.

Numáncia ★★★
Numáncia 74
08029 **Barcelona**
Tel. 322 44 51; fax 410 76 42
140 rooms.

Rallye ★★★
Travessera de les Corts 150
08028 **Barcelona**
Tel. 339 90 50
73 rooms. Swimming pool.

Regente ★★★★
Rambla de Catalunya 76
08007 **Barcelona**
Tel. 215 25 70; tlx. 51939
78 rooms. Swimming pool.

Royal ★★★★
Rambla 117
08002 **Barcelona**
Tel. 301 94 00; tlx. 97565;
fax 317 31 79
*108 rooms. Central location.
Picturesque setting.*

Suizo ★★★
Plaça de l'Àngel 12
08002 **Barcelona**
Tel. 315 41 11; tlx. 97206;
fax 315 38 19
50 rooms. Central location.

Terminal ★★★
Provença 1
08029 **Barcelona**
Tel. 321 53 50; tlx. 98213
75 rooms.

Tres Torres ★★★
Calatrava 32–34
08017 **Barcelona**
Tel. 417 73 00; tlx. 54990;
fax 418 98 34
56 rooms.

LOWER-PRICED
(up to ptas. 10,000)

Bonanova Park ★★
Capità Arenas 51
08013 **Barcelona**
Tel. 204 09 00; tlx. 54990;
fax 204 50 14
60 rooms.

Cortés ★★
Santa Ana 25
08002 **Barcelona**
Tel. 317 92 12; tlx. 98215;
fax 301 31 35
46 rooms. Central location.

Covadonga ★★★
Avda. Diagonal 596
08036 **Barcelona**
Tel. 209 55 11; tlx. 93394;
fax 209 58 33
76 rooms.

España ★★
Sant Pau 9–11
08026 **Barcelona**
Tel. 318 17 58
84 rooms.

Gaudí ★★★
Nou de la Rambla 12
08001 **Barcelona**
Tel. 317 90 32; tlx. 50111
71 rooms. Central location.

Ginebra ★
Rambla de Catalunya 1
08007 **Barcelona**
Tel. 317 10 63
10 rooms.

Gran Via ★★★
Gran Via de les Corts
Catalanes 642
08007 **Barcelona**
Tel. 318 19 00
*48 rooms. Picturesque, central
location. Historic building.*

Lleó ★★
Pelai 24 – 08001 **Barcelona**
Tel. 318 13 12; tlx. 98338
42 rooms. Central location.

Park Hotel ★
Avda. Marquès de l'Argentera 11
08003 **Barcelona**
Tel. 319 60 00
95 rooms.

Regencia Colón ★★★
Sagristans 13–17
08002 **Barcelona**
Tel. 318 98 58; tlx. 98175;
fax 317 28 22
*55 rooms. Central location.
Historic building.*

San Agustín ★★
Plaça de Sant Agustí 3
08001 **Barcelona**
Tel. 317 28 82; tlx. 98121
*70 rooms. Picturesque, central
location.*

Toledano ★
Rambla 138 – 08002 **Barcelona**
Tel. 329 50 15
17 rooms. Central location.

Via Augusta ★★
Via Augusta 63
08006 **Barcelona**
Tel. 217 92 50
44 rooms.

RESTAURANTS

HIGHER-PRICED
(over ptas. 4,000)

Ara-Cata
Doctor Ferràn 33
08034 **Barcelona**
Tel. 204 10 53
*Notably good French and
Catalan cuisine. Discreetly
elegant. Closed Sat.*

Azulete
Via Augusta 281
08017 **Barcelona**
Tel. 203 59 43
*Notably good cuisine. Flowered
terrace. Closed Sat. lunch and
Sun.*

Bel Air
Córcega 286 – 08008 **Barcelona**
Tel. 237 75 88
Rice specialities. Closed Sun.

Botafumeiro
Gran de Grácia 81
08012 **Barcelona**
Tel. 218 42 30
*Seafood specialities. Notably
good cuisine. Closed Sun.
evening and Mon.*

La Cúpula
Teodora Roviralta 37
08022 **Barcelona**
Tel. 212 48 88/418 51 41
*Market cuisine. Ancient tower.
Spacious terrace-garden.*

Eldorado Petit
Dolors Monserdà 51
08017 **Barcelona**
Tel. 204 51 53

*Excellent Catalan cuisine.
Pleasant restaurant. Outdoor
dining. Closed Sun.*

Finisterre
Avda. Diagonal 469
08036 **Barcelona**
Tel. 239 55 76
Excellent cuisine and service.

Florian
Bertrand i Serra 20 (esquina
Mandri)
08022 **Barcelona**
Tel. 212 46 27
*Excellent cuisine. Reservations
essential. Closed Sun.*

Jaume de Provença
Provença 88
08029 **Barcelona**
Tel. 230 00 29
*Notably good cuisine. Closed
Sun. evening and Mon.*

Neichel
Avda. de Pedralbes 16 bis
08034 **Barcelona**
Tel. 203 84 08
*Excellent cuisine. One of the best
restaurants in Spain. Closed Sun.*

Orotava
Consell de Cent 335
08007 **Barcelona**
Tel. 302 31 28
*Game specialities. Notably good
cuisine.*

Reno
Tuset 27
08006 **Barcelona**
Tel. 200 91 29
Excellent cuisine. Very elegant.

Vía Veneto
Ganduxer 10–2
08021 **Barcelona**
Tel. 200 72 44
Considered the best restaurant in
Barcelona. Belle Epoque decor.
Closed Sat. lunch and Sun.

MEDIUM-PRICED
(ptas. 3–4,000)

Aitor
Carbonell 5 (Barceloneta)
08003 **Barcelona**
Tel. 319 94 88
Basque cuisine. Closed Sun.

Amaya
Rambla de Santa Mònica 24
08002 **Barcelona**
Tel. 302 10 37
Catalan-Basque cuisine.

Brasserie Flo
Jonqueres 10
08003 **Barcelona**
Tel. 317 80 37
French and Catalan cuisine.
Excellent quality.

Can Majó
Almirall Aixada 23 (Barceloneta)
08003 **Barcelona**
Tel. 310 14 55/319 50 96
Rice and seafood specialities.
Good cuisine. Closed Mon.

Los Caracoles
Escudellers 14
08002 **Barcelona**
Tel. 301 20 41
Regional country-style decor.

Casa Isidro
Les Flors 12
08001 **Barcelona**
Tel. 241 11 39
Frequented by artists and actors.
Closed Sun.

La Dorada
Travessera de Gràcia 44–46
08021 **Barcelona**
Tel. 200 63 22
Andalusian seafood specialities.
Closed Sun.

Gargantua i Pantagruel
Aragon 214
08011 **Barcelona**
Tel. 253 20 20
Good value. Closed Sun.

Garum
Avda. Marqués de Comillas s/n
(Poble Espanyol)
08004 **Barcelona**
Tel. 423 03 15
Catalan cuisine. Excellent view.
Closed Sun. and Mon. evening.

Gorría
Diputació 421
08013 **Barcelona**
Tel. 245 11 64
Excellent Basque-Navarre
cuisine. Reservations essential.
Closed Sun.

El Gran Café
Avinyó 9
08002 **Barcelona**
Tel. 318 79 86
French and Catalan cuisine.
Piano music in the evening.
Closed Sun.

A la Menta
Passeig Manuel Girona 50
08034 **Barcelona**
Seafood. Closed Sun. evening.

La Odisea
Copons 7
08002 **Barcelona**
Tel. 302 36 92
Good cuisine. Tasteful decor.
Closed Sat. lunch and Sun.

Siete Puertas
Passeig d'Isabel II 14
08003 **Barcelona**
Tel. 319 30 33
Notably good cuisine. Piano
music in the evening.

LOWER-PRICED
(up to ptas. 3,000)

Agut
Gignàs 16
08002 **Barcelona**
Tel. 315 17 09
Catalan cuisine. Closed Sun.
evening.

Antigua Casa Solé
Sant Carles 4 (Barceloneta)
08003 **Barcelona**
Tel. 319 50 12
Seafood specialities.

Can Culleretes
Quintana 5
08002 **Barcelona**
Tel. 317 30 22
Oldest restaurant in Barcelona.
Excellent value. Closed Sun.
evening and Mon.

Can Jaume
Avda. Pau Casals 10
08021 **Barcelona**
Tel. 200 63 58
Home-style cooking. Excellent
value. Closed Sat. evening.

Giardinetto Notte
La Granada del Penedès 22
08006 **Barcelona**
Tel. 218 75 36
Italian Cuisine. Open evening
only until 2.30 a.m. Closed Sun.

Marcos
Buenavista 10
08012 **Barcelona**
Tel. 237 60 99
Good cuisine. Friendly atmos-
phere. Closed Sat. evening
and Sun.

L'Olivé
Muntaner 171
08036 **Barcelona**
Tel. 230 90 97/322 98 47
Catalan cuisine. Outdoor dining.
Reservations essential.
Closed Sun.

Racó d'en Jaume
Provença 98
08029 **Barcelona**
Tel. 239 78 61
Catalan cuisine. Good value.
Closed Sun. evening and Mon.

Sa Lletuga
Mozart 4
08012 **Barcelona**
Tel. 237 96 31
Good cuisine. Closed Sun. and
Mon.

BERLITZ®

BARCELONA

By the staff of Berlitz Guides

How to use this guide

- All the practical information, hints and tips that you will need before and during the trip start on page 104.

- For general background, see the sections The City and the People, page 6, and A Brief History, page 13.

- All the sights to see are listed between pages 23 and 91. Our own choice of sights most highly recommended is pinpointed by the Berlitz traveller symbol.

- Sports, shopping, nightlife and festivals are described from pages 92 to 98, while information on restaurants and cuisine is to be found between pages 99 and 103.

- Finally, there is an index at the back of the book, pages 126 to 128.

Found an error or an omission in this Berlitz Guide? Or a change or new feature we should know about? Our editor would be happy to hear from you. Be sure to include your name and address, since in appreciation for a useful suggestion, we'd like to send you a free travel guide. Write to: Berlitz Publishing Co. Ltd., London Road, Wheatley, Oxford OX9 1YR, England.

Although we make every effort to ensure the accuracy of all the information in this book, changes occur incessantly. We cannot therefore take responsibility for facts, prices, addresses and circumstances in general that are constantly subject to alteration.

Text: Donald Allan
Staff Editor: Christina Jackson
Layout: Doris Haldemann
Photography: Claude Huber
We are grateful to Alfred Bosch, Carlos Sentis, and the staff of the Patronato Municipal de Turismo in Barcelona for their help in the preparation of this guide. We would also like to thank C. von Brentano, Lydia Azaguri, Victoria Béguelin, Parul Subramanian and Dominika von Zahn for invaluable assistance.
Cartography: 🔲 Falk-Verlag, Hamburg

Contents

Cover photo: The spires of the Sagrada Família; photo pp. 2–3 Plaça Reial

The City and the People

Barcelona is a sophisticated city where the creative energy of modern Europe and the seductive pleasures of the Mediterranean meet in happy union. No one would ever call Barcelona provincial. It is definitely a capital, though now of a culture rather than a country. It may be the second city of Spain, but it is the heart and soul of Catalonia, and it ruled an empire before Spain was born.

Protected by the encircling Collserola hills, the city of Barcelona spills down a gentle slope to the sea. Everything seems to happen on the street in full view, from business deals to courting. Or in the bars open to the street in every block. Avenues are broad and leafy, with plazas, fountains and statuary at the main intersections. Few skyscrapers destroy the human scale of the city profile. The buildings built to impress are usually banks, almost as numerous as bars, and a reminder that business pays for Barcelona's beauty.

Your first walk down the famous Rambla, half promenade and half bazaar, plunges you into the centre of things. Throngs of Barcelonans are sightseeing here, too, so visitors fit right in. The Rambla axis will be your point of orientation by day and by night. Ahead is the seaport, to the left is the cathedral and warren of medieval streets, behind is the rectangular grid of 19th-century city planning and the exuberant architecture of Barcelona's unique *Modernisme*, as the Catalans call the city's nationalist interpretation of Art Nouveau. Far to the right rises Montjuïc, hub of the 1992 Olympics, of great art museums, parks, playgrounds and the florid buildings of a world's fair. This monument to Catalan optimism opened in 1929, just before the stockmarket crash.

The fairs of 1888 and 1929 marked bursts of renewal which periodically thrust Barcelona into new orbits of growth and change, just as the remnants of three rings of concentric walls mark early stages of expansion from the ancient Roman citadel. The 1992 Olympic Games have had the same effect. In the last decade of the 20th century, Barcelona is undergoing a renaissance that will boost it into the next

Forward-looking Barcelona, ever youthful amid past glories, is Spain's most European city.

The bar in Barcelona is office, club, café and front row seat.

millennium ahead of time. Selection of the city in 1986 as the site of the 25th Olympiad set off a multi-billion-dollar building boom that goes far beyond **8** the requirements of the games.

New highways speed traffic around the centre, the airport is being upgraded, new transport and entertainment facilities, new parks, museums, concert halls, hotels and office buildings are rising and new housing is reviving rundown neighbourhoods. Tunnels are spearheading an expansion of the

archaeological sites you can visit beneath the old Royal Palace. Above this layer is the Barri Gòtic, the walled medieval quarter, very much alive and lived in continuously for over a thousand years. The Eixample, or Expansion, district, laid out when the walls came down in the 19th century, includes the landmark buildings of Modernisme, as well as fashionable boutiques, galleries, restaurants, hotels and residential blocks. The Diagonal boulevard cuts the city in half, dividing the older, lower districts from what once were villages at the foot of the hills. These have been absorbed by Barcelona but retain their names—Horta, Gràcia, Sarrià, Pedralbes—and some of their individuality. The fast-growing university district boasts the most modern buildings, and beyond it on the outer ring are the factories that have made the city powerful and prosperous.

city on the other side of its confining hills. The upheaval has spread a spirit of excitement, pride and optimism.

Whatever emerges from these changes will be added to several very different Barcelonas of the past. The stones of the Roman city can be seen in columns and walls, and in the

Street signs and menus will tell you right away that Barcelona is different from the rest of Spain. Those words with all the x's are Catalan, the language that embodies the separateness and national pride of the 7 million Catalan-speaking people, from Perpignan in France to Valencia and the **9**

Balearic Islands. Barcelona is the capital of the Autonomous Region of Catalonia, and though both Catalan and Spanish are official languages and most Catalans speak both, the regional government is vigorously promoting Catalan. Over the centuries, outside forces have repeatedly tried—and failed—to suppress Catalan individuality. The most ruthless suppression came during the Franco dictatorship after the 1936–39 Spanish Civil War when Barcelona was a Republican stronghold. Following Franco's death in 1975 Catalonia regained a measure of autonomy and is enthusiastically rediscovering its culture.

Just over half of the 6 million Catalans live in Barcelona's metropolitan area. The city proper counts 1.7 million inhabitants, about half of them immigrants or the children of immigrants from the south and other parts of Spain who have come in search of jobs. Many of the people a visitor is most likely to deal with—taxi drivers, hotel and restaurant employees—do not speak Catalan as their mother tongue. Any Spanish remembered from your school days will be useful. But a few courtesy phrases in Catalan will certainly earn you a smile of appreciation.

Barcelona is not only proud of its language, it also boasts a thousand-year-old parliament, an industrial base that produces close to one-fifth of Spain's output, rich monuments of art from antiquity to Gaudí, Miró and Picasso, swinging entertainment and a mild climate that attracts millions of sun-seekers from the north the year round. The Olympics cap Barcelona's reputation as a sports-minded community that supports championship golf courses, a top football club, sailing from the harbour and skiing only a few hours away in the Pyrenees. The golden beaches and turquoise waters of the Costa Dorada and Costa Brava are within easy reach.

Eating, however, is the true local pastime. Barcelonans seem to be eating at all hours of the day and night. And you too will find it hard to resist the temptation of mounds of seafood, clouds of creamy pastries, and ranks of little snack-filled dishes called *tapas* lined up on the counters of bars. Don't fight it, join the club. Around 11 a.m., a seat at a café table with a *cafe con leche* or a good

The Palau de la Música Catalana's staid brick frame is overwhelmed, inside and out, by exuberant art.

local beer and a few plates of *tapas* is the break you'll need to keep going until the customary 2 p.m. lunch hour. Follow with a quick siesta until shops and museums reopen at 4–4.30 p.m., and by 6 or 7 p.m. you'll be ready to join the crowds lining the snack bars for another nibble to keep your strength up until 9.30 p.m., the earliest that many restaurants serve dinner. Barcelonans burn up a lot of calories in animated conversation at table. They expect at least a three-course meal, with hefty helpings and no nonsense about *nouvelle cuisine*.

At night, another city emerges. The churches, palaces and monuments are illuminated, fountains dance in veils of colour, and the city's heart beats to a different rhythm. Discotheques, cabarets and the Rambla are crowded until very late.

Barcelonans are a handsome and friendly people, deeply democratic. The city has long drawn on the trades, professions and commercial sectors for leadership. The national dance, the *sardana,* is symbolic. Men, women and children holding hands form a circle to perform the intricate steps. There are no solos, but a strong sense of solidarity. People spontaneously dance the *sardana* at all festivals and important occasions as if to say, "We are Catalans. You can join our circle, but you cannot break it."

Barcelona at a Glance

Population: Municipality 1.7 million; metropolitan area 3.5 million. Barcelona is Spain's second largest city after Madrid, and the capital of the Autonomous Region of Catalonia.

Government: The parliament of Catalonia sits in Barcelona; the executive branch of the regional government, the Generalitat, whose head is the President, also has its seat in Barcelona. The province of Barcelona is one of the four that make up Catalonia. The municipal government is run from the Ajuntament, the City Hall.

Economy: With 16 per cent of Spain's population, Catalonia produces about 20 per cent of the country's Gross National Product, 23 per cent of exports and receives nearly 25 per cent of foreign investment. The biggest employer is the automobile manufacturer, SEAT (owned by Volkswagen). After metallurgy, textiles are the main industrial products.

A Brief History

Tradition holds that Barcelona was first named Barcino after the Carthaginian general and father of Hannibal, Hamilcar Barca, who established a base here in 237 B.C. Phoenicians and Greeks had settled the coast before then and Barcino occupied the site of an earlier Celtiberian settlement called Laie. The Romans defeated the Carthaginians in 206 B.C. and ruled Spain for the next 600 years. Roman law, language and culture took firm root. The Roman citadel in Barcelona, surrounded by a massive wall, occupied high ground where the cathedral and city hall now stand. Christian communities spread through Catalonia beginning in the 1st century A.D.

After sacking Rome in A.D. 410, the Germanic Visigoths swept into Spain. Barcelona became their capital from 531 to 554, when they moved to Toledo. The Moorish invasion from Africa in 711 brought the Visigothic kingdom to an end and Catalonia was briefly overrun. But after their defeat beyond the Pyrenees by the Franks in 732, the Moors withdrew without ever retaining a lasting foothold in Catalonia. Charlemagne's knights pushed in after them and installed themselves at the head of border counties to guard the southern flank of his empire.

One of these feudal lords, Guifré el Pilós, or Wilfred the Hairy, dominated the rest as Count of Barcelona. He founded a dynasty in 878 that ruled for nearly 500 years. Thus, while much of Spain was under Moorish influence, Barcelona and most of Catalonia remained Christian and linked to Europe, a twist of fate that forever determined the distinctly different Catalonian character.

The hairy founding father also gave Catalonia its flag of four vertical red stripes on a gold field, the oldest still in use in Europe. According to legend, the stripes were made in Wilfred's blood, drawn on his shield as an escutcheon by the fingers of the Frankish king after the count had courageously defended his overlord in a battle.

The counts of Barcelona declared their independence when the Frankish king Louis V refused to help repulse Moorish raiders in 988, a date celebrated as Catalonia's birth as a nation-state. It was soon enlarged through marriages and military adventures. Ramon Berenguer III, the Great **13**

(1096–1131), took Mallorca, Ibiza and Tarragona from the Moors and acquired the French county of Provence through his wife. His successor, Ramon Berenguer IV, united Catalonia with neighbouring Aragon by marriage, allowing his son Alfonso II to become the first joint Aragon-Catalan king, ruling the Mediterranean coast all the way to Nice. But much of this was lost by the next king, who picked the losing side—a frequent occurrence in Catalan history—in the French crusade against the heretics of Albi.

Succeeding generations then turned towards conquest of the Mediterranean basin. James I, the Conqueror (1213–76), consolidated control over the Balearic Islands and took Valencia. Barcelona was expanding, so he built a second wall around the 13th-century city. Peter III, also the Great (1276–85), annexed Sicily in 1282. In the next 100 years Barcelona reached the peak of its glory. Its territories included Sardinia, Corsica, Naples, the Roussillon in southern France and briefly Athens, which was taken by the

Under Berenguer III, Catalonia stretched from Nice to Valencia and Mallorca 900 years ago.

Almogavers, mercenaries under the piratical corsair Roger de Flor. Peter IV, the Ceremonious (1336–87), despite loss of a quarter of the city's population to the plague, completed Barcelona's great shipyards, built the impressive Saló del Tinell in the Royal Palace and constructed the third and last wall to encircle his capital, bringing the Rambla inside the fortifications.

These were the centuries of great building in Barcelona which saw the cathedral and other magnificent Gothic palaces and monuments erected. Standing between Europe and the Muslim territories, Barcelona served as a channel for the exchange of scientific knowledge and scholarship. The arts flourished in the cities and monasteries of Catalonia, patronized by a vigorous class of artisans, bankers and merchants, including an important Jewish community. The need for foreign trade encouraged shipbuilding and conquest. The beginnings of democratic institutions appeared with a code of laws, the *Usatges de Barcelona,* in the 11th century, a municipal council with participation of leading citizens called the Consell de Cent, or Council of One Hundred, and in 1283 a parliament or Corts for Catalonia, later to become the Generalitat, the civil government. During this period, Barcelona also drew up the *Llibre del Consolat del Mar,* the foundation of European maritime law.

Barcelona's fate took another decisive turn when the marriage of Ferdinand of Aragon-Catalonia (Ferrán II to the Catalans) to Isabella of Castile joined their two crowns and formed the nucleus of a united Spanish state. Barcelona now was just one of the seats of Los Reyes Católicos, called "The Catholic Monarchs" because in 1492 they finally captured the last Moorish redoubt on the Peninsula at Granada. And that same year, as every schoolchild knows, Christopher Columbus discovered America, thanks to financing from the queen. On his return he was received by the monarchs in the Royal Palace in Barcelona.

That was the last Barcelona saw of the New World's riches for 300 years. Exploitation of the discoveries was the monopoly of the queen's country, Castile, which ever since has been the power centre of Spain. In 1494 the administration of Catalonia was placed under Castilian control and the harsh church Inquisition and the **15** expulsion of the Jews was imposed.

The 16th century, a Golden Age for Spain as a whole, saw the political influence of Catalonia and Barcelona decline further. The Dutch-speaking Habsburg grandson of Ferdinand and Isabella became Charles I of Spain in 1516. A few years later he inherited the title of Holy Roman Emperor as Charles V, with challenging duties throughout Europe that gave him little time for Spain. His son Philip II made previously insignificant Madrid the capital of the great Spanish empire and the administrative centre of his country.

As early as 1640 Catalonia declared itself a republic allied to France, with which Spain under Philip IV was then at war. Forced to surrender in 1652, Barcelona saw the Catalan territories north of the Pyrenees delivered to France, fixing the border where it is today. From this point on, Spanish history is a turmoil of constant wars, shifting alliances and disputes over succession to the crown. In these struggles Barcelona automatically sided with whoever was against Madrid, usually ending up the loser.

The worst of these episodes came in the War of the Spanish **16** Succession (1701–1713) be-

tween the backers of Philip of Anjou, the 17-year-old grandson of Louis XIV of France, and the Habsburg claimant, Archduke Charles of Austria. Charles was enthusiastically received when he landed in Catalonia, but Philip, supported by France, won the war and became the first Bourbon ruler as Philip V. After a 13-month siege, on September 11, 1714, Barcelona was captured and sacked by the royal army. The Catalan Generalitat was dissolved and the city's privileges were abolished. The Ciutadella fortress was built to keep the populace subdued, and official use of the Catalan language was outlawed. Typically, Catalonia celebrates this defeat as its national holiday, a symbol of the spirit of resistance.

Trouble for the national government was always an opportunity for the Catalans to rise up—and usually to get slapped down again, as happened frequently in the 19th century. Spain again became a battleground in 1808–1814 between the English and Napoleon's

The palace steps where Ferdinand and Isabella didn't meet Columbus.

troops. Catalonia's national shrine, the monastery at Montserrat, was destroyed by the French. The sequestration of church properties in Spain in 1835 changed the face of Barcelona, as convents were destroyed or closed and replaced by secular buildings and markets.

The spirit of liberalism abroad in Europe reached Spain tardily. After many reverses, a fairly democratic constitution was proclaimed and constitutional monarchy was installed in 1874. Four years later, Barcelona was at long last given the right to trade with the New World colonies. Meanwhile, the city's energies had been directed to industrialization. Spain's first railway in 1875 ran from Barcelona up the coast and later to the French border. The traditional wool trade had developed into booming textile mills. Medieval walls were torn down to make way for an elegant modern district, the Eixample, laid out on a grid of broad avenues where the new industrialists built mansions in the latest fashion—Modernisme. Prosperity was accompanied by a renaissance of interest in Catalan art and literary traditions, *La Renaixença*. In a burst of optimism, **18** the city bid for worldwide recognition at its Universal Exposition of 1888, built on the site of the hated Ciutadella fortress.

An urban working class evolved with industry. Agitation for social justice was added to regionalist ferment. Barcelona became the scene of strikes and anarchist violence. The modern Socialist Party and the UGT, Spain's largest trade union, were both founded in Barcelona at this time. For their part, the industrialists supported Catalan autonomy as a way to be freed from interference by Madrid. In 1914 a union of the four Catalan provinces, Barcelona, Tarragona, Lleida (Lérida) and Girona (Gerona), was formed as the Mancomunitat, with limited autonomy. The region profited from Spanish neutrality in World War I by selling to both sides, further expanding its industry. The Mancomunitat was dissolved in 1924 by General Primo de Rivera who set up a military dictatorship and banned the Catalan language yet again. Despite this setback, an optimistic Barcelona plunged energetically into the preparation of an International Exhibition, with monumental buildings, pavilions and sports facilities erected on the flank of the Montjuïc hill. It opened a few months before the stock-market crash of 1929.

In 1931, general elections brought the Republican party to power. King Alfonso XIII went into exile. The next year Catalonia won a charter establishing home rule, restoration of the regional parliament and flag and recognition of Catalan as the official language of the region. For the next several years the pendulum of power in Spain swung back and forth between Left and Right, provoking violent anarchist and socialist demonstrations and strikes in Barcelona and elsewhere. An attempt to make Catalonia independent was crushed.

The army rebelled in 1936, igniting the bloody Spanish Civil War. Many of Barcelona's churches were put to the torch by anti-clerical mobs. The city was firmly Republi-

Catalan

Catalan is a true language, not a dialect of Castilian Spanish. It developed from spoken Latin during the long Roman rule. Catalan has a rich literature from the 9th century to the present. Its closest relative is Provençal, the defunct tongue of southern France. People who understand French and Spanish can make out a good deal of written and spoken Catalan. But two housewives arguing in a market would be comprehensible only to a native.

Outside Catalonia proper, Catalan is spoken in Valencia, Alicante, the Balearic Islands and north of the French border to Perpignan—some 7 million people in all. It is the official language of Andorra.

In the 18th century, King Philip V tried and failed to abolish Catalan to punish the region for supporting a rival to his throne. General Franco's ruth-less suppression of the language after the Civil War in 1939 only drove it underground and made it a rallying point of opposition. Under the Constitution of 1978 Catalan is recognized as the mother tongue of Catalonia and as the official language of the Autonomous Region, together with Castilian, the official language of Spain.

Mastery of Catalan and Castilian is required for graduation from primary and secondary schools. Most public education is in Catalan, but families can choose to send their children to schools where Castilian is the first language of instruction. Fluent Catalan is required for city and regional government jobs.

It might help to decode all those "x's" if you pronounced them as "ch" or "sh", as in *anxoves* = anchovies. Accent marks show where emphasis falls.

can. In late 1937 it became the capital for a time and a rallying point for the International Brigade. It was one of the last cities to fall to the rebel troops of General Francisco Franco at the war's end in 1939.

During the Civil War some 700,000 men on both sides died on the battlefield, 30,000 were executed or assassinated, including many priests and nuns, and perhaps 15,000 civilians were killed in air raids. Barcelona was repeatedly bombed and its people suffered great hardships.

Catalonia paid a heavy price in defeat. All regional institutions were again abolished and controls from the central government were reimposed. The Catalan language was again proscribed, even in schools and churches. Lluís Companys, President of the Generalitat of Catalonia, and other Republican leaders were executed by Franco's firing squads. For years, Barcelona got little support from Madrid. Nevertheless, its industry recovered and a million or more job-hunters from less prosperous parts of Spain migrated to the Barcelona area. From the 1960s a tourism boom lifted the economy and brought the people of conservative Franco Spain in touch with modern Europe, with Barcelona leading the way.

When Franco died in 1975, the country had already begun to emerge from its isolation. The coronation of his designated successor, Juan Carlos (Joan Carles to the Catalans), the grandson of Alfonso XIII, brought the restoration of parliamentary democracy and a revolutionary relaxation of customs and laws. In the 1978 Constitution, degrees of autonomy were granted to the fractious regions. While a militant Basque minority demanded more independence and resorted to terror tactics, most Catalans were content with the restoration of the Generalitat and regional parliament and the return of Catalan as an official language.

The freeing of controls within the European Community to create a single market finds Barcelona, Spain's industrial engine and bridge to the rest of Europe, poised for a boom and predicting that not only Olympic records will be broken in 1992.

Slicing across the city, the Diagonal boulevard is a showcase of fashionable shops and modern architecture.

20

Historical Landmarks

900–400 B.C.	Celtic tribes settle on peninsula and mix with indigenous Iberians.
237 B.C.	Carthaginian general, Hamilcar Barca, establishes base at Barcino.
206 B.C.	Romans defeat Carthaginians.
1st c. A.D.	Christian settlements spread through Catalonia.
531–554	Barcelona capital of Visigoths.
711	Moorish invasion of Spain.
732	After defeat by Franks, Moors withdraw from Catalonia.
878	Guifré el Pilós (Wilfred the Hairy) founds dynasty of counts of Barcelona.
988	Counts of Barcelona declare independence.
1096–1131	Ramon Berenguer III extends Catalan empire.
1213–1276	James I consolidates empire, expands Barcelona.
1283	Corts (Parliament) of Catalonia established.
1336–1387	Peter IV reigns, builds city's third walls.
1469	Marriage of Ferdinand and Isabella unites Aragon-Catalonia with Castile to create a unified Spain.
1492	Ferdinand and Isabella expel Moors from Spain; Columbus discovers America.
1494	Administration of Catalonia put under Castilian control.
1516	Charles I (Charles V, Holy Roman Emperor) takes throne.
1640	Catalonia declares itself a republic allied to France.
1652	Catalan territories north of Pyrenees ceded to France.
1701–1713	War of Spanish Succession.
1713–1714	Siege of Barcelona by Philip V; Ciutadella fortress built.
1808–1814	Peninsular War between English and Napoleon.
1835	Sequestration of church properties.
1874	Constitutional monarchy installed in Spain.
1888	Universal Exposition in Barcelona.
1914	Mancomunitat formed.
1924	General Primo de Rivera sets up military dictatorship, bans Catalan language.
1929	International Exhibition in Barcelona.
1931	Republican party comes to power.
1932	Catalonia wins home rule.
1936–1939	Spanish Civil War ends in Franco dictatorship.
1975	Franco dies, Juan Carlos becomes king.
1980s	Catalonia achieves autonomy, Catalan language restored.
1986	Spain joins European Community.
1992	Summer Olympics in Barcelona.

What to See

Time, that's the problem. There's a lot to do and see in Barcelona, so planning your day is important. You set out with the best of intentions only to get sidetracked in the colourful maze of a covered market or waylaid by the attractions of a street of antique shops. Then the sight of glistening shrimp on a bed of ice in the doorway of a bar proves irresistible. You sink into a chair at a sidewalk table for a snack, read a newspaper (noting with satisfaction that the weather back home is foul) and before you know it, a church bell strikes noon.

Is it too late to "do" the museum you started out to see? Or too early to ride the aerial cable car across the harbour for lunch at La Barceloneta beach? Decisions, decisions! And what's that archway across the street? The courtyard beyond looks interesting. You step in for a peek and find a small gem of architecture. And time rolls happily on with your plan forgotten. Perhaps it doesn't really matter, as long as you're having a good time. But be forewarned about Barcelona's seductions or you may miss some of the outstanding attractions of this complex and fascinating city.

Very broadly grouped, these are the Barri Gòtic and other medieval districts, the great art museums, spanning the Romanesque period to Picasso, the astonishing architectural fantasies of Gaudí and his contemporaries, and the Rambla with its byways and *tapa* bars. For the purposes of the guide, we have divided Barcelona into easily manageable sections. In the old town, where many streets are too narrow for cars and where a slow pace is rewarded by so many little hidden treasures, the best way to cover the ground is on foot. Each section describing this area is organized in the order of a walking tour, but it is always possible to opt for a different route from the one proposed. For sights further afield, Barcelona has an excellent public transport network—clean, fast and frequent metro trains, modern buses, funiculars and cable cars—as well as plenty of inexpensive taxis.

A good map will be essential, but don't be fooled by how near things look on paper. It's a big city.

La Rambla

Start with the Rambla to immerse yourself in the special Barcelona atmosphere—ener- 23

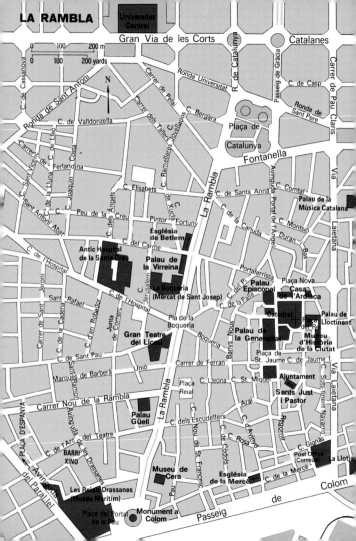

getic, artistic, democratic and indulgent. This broad, tree-shaded promenade stretches nearly 2 kilometres (1 mi.) down a gentle incline from the city's hub, the Plaça de Catalunya (see pp. 58–59), to the waterfront. La Rambla takes its name not from the rambling pace of boulevardiers, but from an Arabic word meaning a sandy, dry river bed, which indeed it originally was. In the 13th century a wall ran alongside the gully with roads on each side, like the streets that today one has to dart across through traffic to reach the central walkway.

There are five sections to the Rambla if you go by the street signs. Actually they merge seamlessly, though as you stroll along, the character and denizens of the Rambla do change. The short **Rambla de Canaletes** at the top is where crowds pour in from the Plaça de Catalunya or come up from the metro and train stations beneath. On Sundays and Mondays in season you'll find knots of gesticulating fans replaying the games of the Barça, Barcelona's beloved football club. This is their recognized turf. Here, too, begin the stalls where you can buy not only foreign newspapers and magazines, often on the day of issue,

Barcelona Mas que Mai!
"Barcelona more than ever!" goes the boasting slogan of the municipality. And Barcelona plans to live up to it in every way. Lest the world forget in the run-up to the Olympics that Barcelona is also a city of art, 1992 and the two preceding years will see a "Cultural Olympiad", a full calendar of special events and prizes organized by the city.

Of lasting importance are the reorganization of the great Museu d'Art de Catalunya on Montjuïc to become the "Catalan Louvre", and the construction of a cultural centre near the now marginal Plaça de les Glòries Catalanes, including a National Theatre and a City Auditorium. In the Raval area behind the Boqueria market, a Centre for Contemporary Culture is to rise. This would house a Modern Art Museum to replace the less than modern one in the Ciutadella Park.

Many historic buildings are being cleared of the accretions and encumbrances of centuries to reappear in their original beauty and be put to cultural uses. Among these are the Casa de la Caritat, now a "cultural laboratory", and the Convento de Los Angeles, to be the library for all the art museums. Even the grand old Liceu will at last be air-conditioned and get modern equipment backstage.

27

but also books, for Barcelona is a centre of publishing. The farther down the Rambla you go, however, the more the publications reflect the relaxation of pornography laws.

The **Rambla dels Estudis** is popularly called the Rambla dels Ocells, "of the birds" because it narrows here to become an outdoor aviary where birds of all descriptions are sold. When the vendors leave, their stalls lined with cages are folded and shut like wardrobes, with the birds rustling about inside. Pigeons flaunt their liberty, scavenging fallen seed and circling over the prisons of their cousins.

Birds give way to blossoms in the Rambla de les Flors, officially the **Rambla de Sant Josep**, the very emblem of Barcelona to the world and probably the most photographed scene in the city. Two products of the Rambla enjoy a brisk trade on April 23, the day of Barcelona's patron, Sant Jordi (St. George), which is celebrated as the Day of the Book and when it is also traditional to give girls a rose. Facing the

"Living statue" draws mixed reviews. Strollers expect the unexpected on La Rambla.

28

"Lane of Flowers" is the elegant **Palau de la Virreina**, a palace completed in 1778 for the widow of the viceroy of colonial Peru. At street level is a service of the city's Department of Culture where tickets to municipal concerts are sold or offered and information about museums and current exhibitions is available.

Set back from the street, a

The secret of Catalan cooking is the freshness of its produce, spread in a carpet of colour at markets like La Boqueria.

giant red pepper stands under a stained-glass medallion hanging over the entrance to the overflowing cornucopia of earthly delights that is the Mercat de Sant Josep, or **La Boqueria**. This is the queen of Barcelona's many magnificent 19th-century covered markets. La Boqueria is a community

where shoppers and merchants greet each other by name, where ribald sallies across the aisles set off gales of laughter, where the freshness of a *rape* (an angler fish popular in Catalonia) is debated with the passion of a traffic mishap. The market is huge, laid out under high-ceilinged ironwork naves, like a railway station. And huge are the heaps of fruit, vegetables, seafood, sausages, meat and poultry, and enough spices, neatly braided ropes of garlic, sun-dried tomatoes and peppers, preserves and sweetmeats to make a gourmet swoon. Restaurants in and near the market are like first-aid stations for those who become faint with hunger at the sight of such riches. The market opens before dawn, but closes down in mid-afternoon. It's at its best in the morning.

The heart of the Rambla is the **Pla de la Boqueria**. The Rambla's busiest intersection broadens here at the market and at the staircase to a metro station. The centre of the *pla* ("square" or "plain" in Catalan) is paved with a mosaic unmistakably by the painter Joan Miró. You'll be coming back again and again to this focal point, whether from walks in the Barri Gòtic, the Gothic quarter to the left **31** (see pp. 34–47), or from exploring El Raval, the district to the right (see pp. 60–63), or perhaps to attend a performance at the doyenne of Spain's opera houses, the **Gran Teatre del Liceu**. A monument of the Catalan *Renaixença* (renaissance) opened in 1847, the Liceu is grand indeed, all gold and red plush, five tiers high, seating 3,500. The season runs from October to June. If you're superstitious, take note: in 1893 an anarchist threw a bomb from the top balcony that exploded in row 13 of the orchestra seats, killing 20 spectators.

Across the way is the venerable **Café del'Opera**, a good spot for a bit of refreshment before you push on down the next stretch, the **Rambla dels Caputxins**. The tone and the incline are both a bit downhill after the Liceu, but the street entertainment starts here. You'll encounter jugglers, fire-eaters, sidewalk artists, including those reproducing masterworks in chalks on the pavement, tarot-card readers, "human statues" who interrupt their frozen pose to salute pretty girls, violinists, lottery-ticket sellers, assorted crackpots and mendicants. Note the naïve painted angels floating **32** over the doorway of the old

Hotel Oriente, which preserves part of the 17th-century cloister of a Franciscan school inside. Just beyond the hotel, around the corner on the Carrer Nou de la Rambla, is the **Palau Güell**, the mansion Gaudí built in 1885 for his principal patron, the textile tycoon Count Eusebi Güell. Gaudí's work will be discussed later on (see pp. 52–59), but a brief detour from the Rambla is in order to see this far from cozy, meticulously detailed fortress-like home, now a theatrical museum.

Returning to the Rambla, cross over and follow the short passage that leads into the arcaded **Plaça Reial**. This handsome and spacious square is graced with a fountain, palm trees and wrought-iron lampposts by the young Gaudí. Like the Boqueria, the Hotel Oriente and other Rambla landmarks, this square came into being as a result of the destruction of a convent when church properties were expropriated in an anti-clerical period of the mid-19th century. Today it is somewhat decayed, best known for the large tankards of beer served at its cafés and for a stamp and coin market held on Sunday mornings.

The final promenade leading to the harbour is the short **Rambla de Santa Mònica**,

METRO

Metro Linia 1
Metro Linia 3
Metro Linia 4
Metro Linia 5

Ferrocarrils
Tramvia Blau
Funicular
Telefèric

beginning at the Plaça del Teatre, site of the run-down Teatre Principal. The area is the beat of prostitutes and cops on the lookout for pickpockets and bag-snatchers. The warren of alleys to the right is the **Barri Xino**, or Chinatown, once notorious for forbidden sin. Now that many erstwhile sins are no longer forbidden, it has lost much of its interest and customers, though it's still no place for a midnight stroll. The **Carrer dels Escudellers** on the other side of the Rambla is the gateway to a district of cabarets, bars, flamenco shows and restaurants, including the well-known Los Caracoles where chickens are turning on spits on the street corner.

Nearer the port, a passage leads to the **Museu de Cera** (Wax Museum). It's very well done. You get the feeling someone is watching you, turn around, and it's Einstein, Maria Callas or one of 300 other effigies. There's an astronaut in the space section and a fairly gory chamber of horrors. The Rambla ends at the broad open space of the **Plaça del Portal de la Pau** (Gate of Peace Square) and the Monument a Colom, in honour of Columbus (Colom in Catalan). This is also the starting point for walks along the waterfront (see pp. 63–69).

Barri Gòtic

Barcelona has grown outwards in rings from its beginnings more than 2,000 years ago, like concentric ripples on a pond. The ancient core is a hill the Romans called Mons Taber where they raised a temple to Augustus Caesar and in the 4th century built high walls about a mile around to protect their settlement. The Visigoths and Frankish rulers who followed also lived within the first ring, the nucleus of the medieval district called the Barri Gòtic. In the 1940s the clutter of buildings that over the centuries had encrusted this centre like barnacles on a ship were removed. The best were dismantled and relocated. The walls and main palaces were thus restored to view and the district has become the main attraction for visitors, as well as a lively centre of administration, commerce and art for Barcelona.

Taking off again from the Plaça de Catalunya, follow the Avinguda del Portal de l'Àngel past the Galerías Preciados department store to the **Col.legi d'Arquitectes**

Keep looking overhead: in the Barri Gòtic there's a surprise at every turn.

(College of Architects). The period in Col.legi is a Catalan punctuation that indicates a stretching of the "L" sound. Picasso contributed the drawings of the Three Kings and the children bearing palm branches engraved on the modern façade. The theme perhaps alludes to the street market that sells Christmas crib figurines from December 8–24 around the corner in the **Plaça Nova**—a square that got its name, meaning "new", in 1356. This open space has held markets for nearly a thousand years. These days antique dealers set up stalls every Thursday in front of the steps between two towers of the Roman wall.

To get the mood of the old fortified core, follow the walls for a bit, passing in front of the cathedral, which generally is blocked from the street by a restless herd of tour buses, and continue along the Carrer de la Tapineria. This leads to the **Plaça de Berenguer el Gran**, whose statue on horseback seems small beside the well-preserved section of wall at this point. The Roman defences are 9 metres (30 ft.) high and 3.5 metres (11.8 ft.) thick and were marked at intervals by towers 18 metres (60 ft.) tall. Until 1943, most of this section was covered by old houses built against the walls.

The Baixada de la Llibreteria crosses the wall line into the Barri Gòtic and the first turning to the right leads immediately to the **Museu d'Història de la Ciutat** (Museum of History of the City). The building is a Gothic mansion that was moved stone by stone to this location. Its exhibits are worth visiting early in your stay to get your bearings and some historical perspective.

Go first to the basement, where excavations have uncovered sculpture, streets, house walls, a bathing pool, drains and cemeteries of the Roman and even pre-Roman Mons Taber. Then proceed to the upper floors where you'll see maps of the Catalan empire at its height, with consulates all around the Mediterranean, from Tripoli to Tyre. Another series of maps and engravings shows the 1713–14 siege of Barcelona by Philip V and how the walls were breached. A flag of the Guild of Gardeners emblazoned with pruning knives, hoes and other humble tools, a collection of tiles illustrating medieval occupations and a family tree of trades are marks of the respect for business that has characterized Barcelona from its beginnings and also evidence of the prestige of the craft guilds in the Middle Ages. A huge iron and wood clockworks on display was made in 1575 and weighs 5,512 kg. (12,000 lbs). It told time and rang the cathedral bells for 300 years. Here too are the original plans for the 19th-century expansion of the city that created the Eixample district beyond the old walls.

From the museum it is a step to the Plaça del Rei, the courtyard of the **Palau Reial** (Royal Palace) dominated by the many-arched lookout tower of King Martin and, atop the Roman walls, the **Capella de Santa Àgata** (Chapel of St. Agatha). The chapel is notable for the 15th-century altarpiece of the *Adoration of the Magi* by one of Catalonia's finest artists, Jaume Huguet. Note the slim St. George standing proudly on a lizard-like dragon no bigger than a doormat. St. Agatha was martyred by having her breasts cut off. A curious painting shows the unruffled saint holding them on a plate, looking like buns. In the courtyard, the structure with the broad staircase is all that is left of the Royal Palace of Catalonia, probably begun in the 10th century and added to over the years until it took up three sides of the square and extended to the rear. During the Inquisition, suspected heretics were burned at the stake in this enclosure, and here Ferdinand and Isabella received Columbus on his return from his first voyage in 1493. That historic meeting, of which unfortunately no contemporary account survives, did not take place on the stairs, as romantic paintings would have us believe, because they weren't there for another 50 years or so.

Columbus probably gave his report in the **Saló del Tinell**. This vast barrel-vaulted hall was built for royal audiences in 1359 and on occasion the Catalan Corts (parliament) met here. The walls were once decorated with murals, a fragment of which is preserved in the city museum.

The palace's central section, chapel and hall were reconstructed between 1943–52. Outdoor theatre and concerts are held in the square in summer. It looks its best at night, with lights picking out the arches and the half-darkness giving imagination full rein.

A former wing of the palace which encloses the Plaça del Rei was rebuilt in 1557 to become the **Palau del Lloctinent** (Palace of the Lieutenant), residence of the king's representative. It now houses the **37**

Archives of Aragon. The entrance, reached by leaving the palace square and turning right on the Carrer dels Comtes, is an elegant patio with a noble staircase and remarkable carved wooden ceiling. The intriguing bronze door on the staircase is by the modern Barcelona artist Nùria Fedra. A few steps farther on is the tiny Plaça de Sant Iu, adorned with the Renaissance doorway that once stood at the top of the Royal Palace stairs. Down a few steps is a courtyard with benches amid bits and pieces of ruins and the entrance to the **Museu Frederic Marés**.

Frederic Marés was a competent 20th-century sculptor of civic statues, but he will be best remembered as a compulsive collector who gave Barcelona one of the most idiosyncratic, magpie collections of art and miscellany ever brought under one roof. The lower floors are notable for Iberian votive figurines, Limoges enamel boxes, the Romanesque portal of a church from Huesca, and a sampling of religious sculptures from the 12th to 19th centuries. Among these on the sec-

ond floor is a lovely 15th-century painted English *Virgen de la Misericordia*. Continuing upstairs, the collection changes abruptly. Portuguese carved and painted ox yokes, a roomful of iron keys, old sewing machines, framed collages of cut-out Valentines, more shoes than Imelda Marcos collected, more fans than Sally Rand's, and hat pins, shoe buckles, scissors, dolls' dresses, silver baby rattles, cigar bands, ash trays, cameras, clocks, razors, stereopticon views, canes, lead soldiers, music boxes, bicycles, bed warmers, wind-up toys... the catalogue is endless. There is even the suitcase, covered with travel stickers, in which Marés brought home his loot.

Retracing your steps on the narrow street flanking the cathedral, circle around it to the rear and duck into the narrow Carrer del Paradís. Here, just inside the doorway of the **Centre Excursionista de Catalunya**, four columns of the Roman Temple of Augustus are embedded in the wall.

Behind the cathedral apse, in the Carrer de la Pietat, stands a good example of a 14th-century Catalan house, the **Casa dels Canonges**. This former chapter house of the cathedral canons was restored in 1929 for official use. Next comes a small open **39**

The final touch, the Gothic façade, was added to the cathedral in 1892.

space where musicians, like the troubadours of old, play for contributions beside the Flamboyant Gothic **Porta de la Pietat** cathedral door noted for a Flemish carved wooden panel above its lintel.

Here the street leads into the Carrer del Bisbe Irurita which in turn brings you to the Carrer de Santa Llúcia. To the left is the **Palau Episcopal**, the 18th-century Baroque Bishop's Palace, with an austere courtyard; the more appealing **Casa de l'Ardiaca**, once the archdeacon's residence, has a curious marble letterbox panel of swallows and a tortoise, a 19th-century contribution of the modernist architect Domènech i Montaner. Inside, an informal patio is decorated with brightly coloured floral tiles, a mossy fountain and the cool green shade of a palm.

And now you finally approach the front of the **Catedral de Santa Eulàlia**. The platform between its portico and the steps leading down to the Plaça Nova and the Avinguda de la Catedral is the Pla de la Seu, where impromptu dancing of the *sardana* takes place on Sundays and holidays. The Gothic buildings on the far side of the steps have been restored. Where a hundred poor persons a day were once fed at a medieval almshouse there are now souvenir shops.

The cathedral was begun in 1298 on the site of earlier churches going back to Visigothic times. The final touch, the rather florid Gothic façade, was not completed until 1892 and contrasts with the simple octagonal towers. Its cool, dark interior and leafy cloister offer welcome relief from the heat and glare of a summer's day. The ribs of the high vault are joined at carved and painted keystone medallions, a typically Catalan feature. In the centre of the nave is a Gothic choir with lacy spires of carved wood over each seat. Above these are the heraldic emblems of the European kings and princes invited by Charles V to be members of his exclusive Order of the Golden Fleece *(Toison d'Or)*. The first and only meeting of the local chapter was held in the cathedral in 1519. The seats reserved for Henry VIII of England and François I of France are next to the emperor's, but they did not show up for the party.

Connected to the choir is a pulpit with an exceptional wrought-iron stair rail. Ahead, steps under the altar lead to the alabaster tomb of Santa Eulàlia, one of the city's two patron saints, martyred for her faith

Raw realism and roses: two sides of faith in cathedral cloister.

in the 4th century. Notice the angel choir of plump stone heads around the stairway and crypt arch—actually portraits of royalty who attended the transfer of her remains here in 1339. On the wall of the right aisle are the tombs of Count Ramon Berenguer I and his wife Almodis who founded the earlier cathedral on this spot in 1058—both of them very short, it seems. Don't miss the Catalan Gothic paintings in the chapels behind the altar. The nine panels of the Transfiguration painted for the San Benito chapel in the 15th century by Bernat Martorell are considered his masterpiece, but they are poorly lit and hard to see through the chapel bars.

The **cloister** is a-twitter with birds fluttering in the orange, magnolia and palm trees that entirely fill its centre and pervaded by the honking of geese, guardians of the premises, waddling around a fountain. The cloister is paved with tombstones, badly worn, but many still visibly bearing the emblems of the bootmakers, tailors and other craft guilds whose wealth helped pay for **41** the cathedral. One chapel is dedicated to 930 priests and nuns of the diocese killed in the anticlerical slaughter of the 1936–39 Civil War. From the cloister, pass to the **Capella de Santa Llúcia** (Chapel of St. Lucy), with more 13th- and 14th-century tombstones on the floor and the monument to a crusader knight in armour on a wall. The little lap dogs at the feet of such memorials always seem very tame pets for warriors.

Leaving the Capella de Santa Llúcia by its front entrance, turn left at the Carrer del Bisbe Irurita. The corner house at No. 8 was the official residence of the President of the Generalitat until recently. Keep looking upwards as you walk through the old town. There's always something interesting to see, a curious hanging sign or lantern, a bit of sculpture or a brilliant design produced by lines of laundry looped this way and that overhead. Here on the right you'll find a row of gargoyles leaning from the roof of the Palau de la Generalitat, the seat of government for the Autonomous Region of Catalonia, and a richly ornamented gateway. Above it is a marvellous medallion with Sant Jordi (St. George) on a kind of merry-go-round horse looking as though

he were hanging onto a carousel, not slaying a dragon. The lacy overhead bridge is a 1929 addition that fits in well.

Back down Carrer del Bisbe Irurita you emerge into the spacious **Plaça de Sant Jaume**, the heart of the Barri Gòtic. A local joke says that the farthest distance in Barcelona is across this square, which separates the often antagonistic Generalitat and the municipal authorities in the Ajuntament, the City Hall. Together they must haggle with Madrid, for the central government collects the main taxes, returning a share to the region. Then a further slicing of the pie and decisions on who pays for what brings confrontations that are exacerbated when the two are run by different political parties. Barcelona is socialist and the regional authority is traditionally more conservative. In any case, the two buildings make a harmonious pair architecturally. Both have classical façades that hide their Gothic origins.

The **Palau de la Generalitat** is the more interesting of the two. This institution dates from 1359, when it was made the executive branch reporting to the parliament, the Corts of Catalonia. The nucleus of the present building is the main patio of purest Catalan Gothic,

42

with its open staircase leading to a gallery of arches on slender pillars. In 1526 the unusual upper patio was added. It is planted with orange trees whose perfume undermines the bureaucratic atmosphere in spring. It is a tranquil spot where, at midday, the bells of the campanile are played. The jewel of the building is the sumptuous Flamboyant Gothic façade of the **Capella de Sant Jordi**. You can't get away from St. George here. The **Saló de Sant Jordi**, a large vaulted hall in the 17th-century front block of the building, is lined with modern murals of historical scenes. In the past, the palace has indeed had its ups and downs. The Generalitat was abolished in 1714 by Philip V, who made the building a court. This remained until 1908, when it was the seat of the crown's provincial authorities until the brief period of autonomy under the 1931–39 Republic. A provincial office again during the Franco years, it finally welcomed back the revived Generalitat in 1977.

The **Ajuntament**, or Casa de la Ciutat, across the way has been Barcelona's city hall since 1372. It was here that the Consell de Cent, a council of 100 notable citizens, met to deal with civic affairs under the watchful eyes of the king. The original entrance can be seen around the left-hand corner of the building, on the Carrer de la Ciutat. The very official-looking new façade was erected in 1845. Inside, the left staircase leads to the upper gallery of the old courtyard and to the **Saló de Cent** (Hall of the One Hundred). Its high ceiling resembles the barrel-vault of the Saló del Tinell and was built at about the same time in the 14th century. The red and yellow bars of Catalonia's flag decorate the walls. The hall where the city council now meets adjoins, and at the head of the black marble staircase is the **Saló de les Cròniques** (Hall of the Chronicles), noted for the modern murals in sepia tones by Josep Maria Sert. The fellow with the knife in his back is Roger de Flor, the Catalan corsair who was assassinated during the campaign depicted here when his mercenaries took Athens (see pp. 14–15).

From behind the Ajuntament, take the short Carrer d'Hèrcules to the **Plaça de Sant Just** for a look at the church of **Sants Just i Pastor**. The small square is enough off the beaten track and lacking in "improvements" to preserve the flavour of a bygone Barcelona. There's a fountain installed in 1367 that **43** is still in use (with new fixtures). The church is one of the oldest in the city, though often remodelled. Since the 10th century any will sworn to before the church's altar is recognized as valid by the courts of Barcelona.

Since ancient times, when the two main Roman thoroughfares intersected here, the Plaça de Sant Jaume has been the crossroads of Barcelona. Streets radiate in all directions, each an invitation to explore the Barri Gòtic. The Carrer del Call leads into the labyrinth of narrow streets that was the **Call**, or Jewish Quarter until the Jews were expelled in 1492. Today the quarter is almost solid antique shops and dealers in rare books, plus bars and restaurants frequented by antiquarians and artists. Although many of the streets have Call in their names, there are few vestiges left of the ghetto, which once was surrounded by a wall. The Jews of Barcelona, though noted as doctors, scholars and jewellers, and despite their financing of the conquests of the crown, were confined to this district and had to wear long-hooded cloaks with a yellow headband. Taxes on Jews were a special source of royal income, for they were considered to be the personal property of the ruler and as such benefited from royal protection. This did not, however, save the Call from being burned and looted as persecution mounted in the 14th and 15th centuries. Stones from Jewish tombs can be seen in the west wall of the Generalitat and other Barri Gòtic palaces, and just off the Carrer del Call, at No. 1 Carrer de Marlet, a medieval inscription in Hebrew marks the site of a hospital founded by one "Rabbi Samuel Hassareri, may his life never cease".

Farther on is the Baixada de Santa Eulàlia. Local lore holds that the saint was martyred here in 304 by being rolled down the slope in a barrel full of broken glass, though the official record has her done in far across the country, in Mérida. A few steps more bring one into a charming tiny square closed to traffic where kids love to play football. This is the **Plaça de Sant Felip Neri**. The saint's church was pockmarked by Italian bombs during the Civil War. To the right are two houses of medieval guilds, first the **Casa dels Calderers** (House of the Cauldron-Makers), and then

Designs are scraped in plaster on 18th-century bourgeois house fronts.

the **Casa Gremial dels Sabaters** (House of the Shoemakers), which contains a small museum of footwear, including some high-button shoes of Pau (Pablo) Casals. Both buildings were moved here during the construction of streets that opened up the Barri Gòtic beyond the cathedral.

The Baixada de Santa Eulàlia descends to the **Carrer dels Banys Nous**, named for the long-gone "new" baths of the ghetto erected in the 12th century. This curving street more or less follows the line of the old Roman wall and is the unofficial boundary of the Barri Gòtic. Keep your eyes peeled as you walk along for odd hand-painted shop signs, the fretwork of Gothic windows and treasures (or reasonable facsimiles) in the antique shop windows. You'll see the old tile signs with a cart symbol high in the walls at some corners, the indication of one-way streets. Within the walls in the 19th century, Barcelona had more than 200 streets less than 3 metres (10 ft.) wide.

Forge ahead into the Plaça de Sant Josep Oriol, which connects with the Plaça del Pi in front of **Santa Maria del Pi**, a handsome church with a tall octagonal bell tower and a harmonious façade pierced by a large rose window completed in 1453. "Pi" means pine tree, and there is a small specimen here replacing one that was a landmark in past centuries. The two adjoining squares, together with the small Placeta del Pi to the rear of the church, are the essence of old Barcelona.

All around, a shifting cast of characters—musicians, puppeteers, pantomimists, hawkers of handicrafts, and panhandlers—vies for attention. Shopkeepers gossip on the doorsteps of once-important buildings whose walls are adorned with allegorical figures in *esgrafiado,* the *sgrafitto* technique imported from Italy in the early 1700s of scraping designs in coloured plaster. (The up-and-coming Barcelona merchant class favoured such façades as an inexpensive substitute for the sculpture found in aristocratic palaces.) A bar with tables under spreading plane trees is a shady oasis by day and equally popular by night, when the church and square are lit up. On Sundays, artists offer their canvases for sale here. A large arcade of shops selling a miscellany of trendy clothes, cassettes and joke items completes the typically Barcelonan mix.

One other tranquil and beautiful corner should be visited before leaving this part of the city, the **Monestir de Santa Anna**. The Carrer de Santa Anna is off the commercial Avinguda del Portal de l'Àngel and it, too, is crowded with shoppers. In a dark archway, banks of bright colour from a flower stand catch the eye and then an open space with trees and benches beckons. The simple lines of a low Romanesque church contrast with the backs of tall office buildings just beyond. In the 11th century, the monastery stood in fields outside the Roman walls. All that's left now is a small cloister and the church and a little island of calm.

Santa Maria del Mar

Some of the most beautiful Gothic architecture and most fascinating medieval corners of Barcelona lie outside the Barri Gòtic. To the east of the Via Laietana—a busy avenue roughly parallel to the Rambla cut through the old city in 1909 to link the port with the modern centre—and below the Carrer de la Princesa, which intersects it at midpoint, is the atmospheric quarter centred on the majestic church of **Santa Maria del Mar** (St. Mary of the Sea). The Carrer Argenteria, once the avenue to the sea from

the Royal Palace, leads straight to the church from the Plaça de l'Àngel. Begun in 1329 at the height of Catalonia's expansion as a Mediterranean power, Santa Maria del Mar is pure Catalan Gothic, with unadorned exterior walls, a flat roof, sober façade flanked by two three-tiered octagonal bell towers and a large rose window over the portal. Fires set alight in the rioting of 1936 at the outbreak of the Civil War consumed all the trappings of chapels, choir and altar, leaving the interior stripped to its essence. The result is a spacious and lofty hall suffused with soft light from stained-glass windows. Three tall naves are supported by slim octagonal columns set 13 metres (43 ft.) apart; the dimensions of the interior are multiples of this distance, achieving a perfect symmetry. Behind the simple modern altar, the columns cluster like stately trees that branch high overhead into the arched vaulting of the apse. The acoustics are excellent for the concerts often held in the church and for the voices of choirboys at mass.

The rear door of the church leads to the **Passeig del Born**, a large open space where jousts were held in the Middle Ages and fairs and festivals take place today. Here you can see

Santa Maria del Mar's simple lines are purest Catalan Gothic.

the bridge over the Carrer de Santa Maria by which the vice-roy of King Carlos III entered the church in the 18th century, avoiding the hostile public. Many of the little streets surrounding the church are named after the crafts-men who once had their shops here or after their products, such as Sombrerers (hatters), Mirallers (mirror-makers), Es-paseria (sword-makers) and Esparteria (rope-soled shoes). Ducking down these alleys leads one back through centuries. The **Carrer de les Caputxes** (hoods) in front of the church is one of the least changed by time. In the short **Carrer del Fossar de les Moreres**, a plaque marks the common grave of men who fell defending the city during the 1713–14 siege of the city. The **Carrer de les Mosques**

48

(it means flies, not Muslim temples) behind the Born on the other side of the church is less than 1.5 metres (5 ft.) wide, the city's narrowest.

Off the Born in the little Plaça de les Olles down the Carrer de la Vidrieria (glass-makers) is a pastry shop founded in 1878 where you can watch goodies being made in a window and then go inside and see if they taste as delicious as they look. At the end of the Passeig del Born is, the large iron and glass shed of **El Born**, the former wholesale market now used for theatrical and musical spectacles. Nearby is the **Homage to Picasso** by Spain's leading abstract artist, Antoni Tàpies. It's a 4-metre (13-ft.) glass cube set in a pool of rushing water. A screen of water running down the inner walls of the cube distorts and makes mysterious the contents—iron rods, and a sofa and chair covered by a dust cloth, as if shut up in an empty house.

Picasso's own museum is reached from the Born by the **Carrer de Montcada,** the most aristocratic street from the 14th to the 16th centuries. It is lined with palaces, each with an imposing door or arched gate to an inner court where an ornamental staircase usually led to reception rooms on the first floor.

These mansions were gradually abandoned after the demolition of the adjoining district and construction of the Ciutadella fortress. Then the business of the port moved closer to the Rambla and the new centre of fashion became the Carrer Ample and the church of La Mercè. The quarter around Santa Maria del Mar, including the Carrer de Montcada, decayed gently without interference, leaving it the most authentically medieval part of the city.

Today the area is enjoying a revival as a neighbourhood of art galleries around the **Museu Picasso**. The Palau Aguilar, a 15th-century mansion, was acquired by the city to house, along with the Palau Castellet, the collection of paintings, drawings and ceramics donated by Picasso's lifelong friend and secretary, Jaume Sabartés. After the museum opened in 1963, Picasso added sketches and paintings from his childhood and youth, as well as the famous 44 variations on the theme of *Las Meninas,* the Velázquez masterpiece in Madrid's Prado Museum. The earliest items date from Picasso's ninth year. Before long he was doing very creditable sketches of his father, mother and sister. And as a teenager he produced large and **49** fully composed canvases in the moralizing 19th-century realist manner, such as the *First Communion* and *Science and Charity*. There follow the sketchbooks from his first visits to Paris and the results of his exposure to the styles of Toulouse-Lautrec, Renoir and others.

As he develops, it is as if he digested the styles of the past and of his contemporaries, proved he could match them, then forged energetically ahead into the future. He is his own man with two good examples of the "Blue Period" (1903) and with the *The Harlequin* (1917). The museum does not attempt

to document each phase of the painter's extraordinary career. The rooms exhibiting the *Las Meninas* series give a fascinating view of Picasso's approach to his subject, taking it apart, emphasizing now this, now that element, experimenting with colour, and with the lack of it. In one version, he brings

Picasso

Pablo Ruiz y Picasso was born in 1881 in Málaga, the son of a drawing teacher whose work took the family to Barcelona, where Picasso demonstrated precocious artistic skill. In 1900 he visited Paris and settled there four years later. Picasso never returned to Barcelona after 1934, and in any case his opposition to the Franco regime would have made this impossible. When Picasso died in 1973, the bulk of his own collection, now in the Musée Picasso in Paris, went to the French government in a deal to settle taxes.

Barcelona's Picassos are nevertheless extremely interesting. It is almost unbelievable that the painter of the saccharine but technically impeccable *First Communion* was a 15-year-old, or that the vigorous lines of the sprawling nudes dated 1972 were the work of a nonagenarian, and that Picasso created both.

Picasso's life and work bridged the 19th and 20th centuries. Even more, it summarized 500 years of painting up to his own arrival and then went on to break new ground that changed forever the way we look at art.

Splendid Renaissance palaces line the Carrer de Montcada.

Velázquez out of the shadowy background of the original and, perhaps in a tribute, has him dominating his picture. Finally, there are rooms dedicated to drawings and lithographs on Picasso-esque subjects: the dove of peace, minotaurs, fauns and nudes. The last is dated 1972, the year before his death, showing the Picasso line as bold and sure as ever. The museum is open from 10 a.m. to 7.30 p.m. and is closed on Mondays. There is a stone-vaulted coffee bar off the patio of the building.

Across the street is the **Museu Tèxtil i de la Indumentària** (Textile and Costume Museum) in the former palace of the Marquesos de Lió. It's a very handsome residence and its collection brings to life the elegance enjoyed by the rich families who occupied such houses. The costumes exhibited are of superb silks, satins and furs, embroidered and stitched to perfection. Styles represented come right down to flapper dresses of the 1920s. The museum is open from 9 a.m. to 2 p.m. and from 4.30 to 7 p.m. Tuesday to Saturday, mornings only on Sundays and holidays. It is closed on Mondays.

The Carrer de la Princesa leads back to the centre of

things and the Via Laietana. Above this street are other points of interest, such as the tiny Romanesque **Capella de Marcús** on the continuation of Carrer de Montcada, and around the corner from it on the Carrer dels Carders, the picturesque courtyard of the **Hostal de la Bona Sort**, or "Good Luck Lodge", once an inn for carters. The heart of this quarter is the **Mercat de Santa Caterina**, a large market square in an untouristy and typically Barcelonan neighbourhood.

L'Eixample

The modern centre of Barcelona is called the "Eixample" in Catalan and the "Ensanche" in Spanish, meaning the Expansion district. It came about all at once in a remarkable burst of urban development that also made the city the showcase of Modernisme in the extravagant architecture of Antoni Gaudí and his peers. By the mid-1800s Barcelona was bursting at the seams and suffocating inside its ring of medieval walls. A competition was held in 1859 to select a plan for a new quarter between the old city and the Collserola hills. After some dispute with Madrid, the job went to a road engineer named Ildefons Cerdà. His plan quintupled the city's size in a matter of decades. It called for a grid of streets with the corners of the blocks cut off to make every intersection spacious. He proposed that construction be on three sides only of each block, leaving the centre and one side for gardens. Several broad avenues connecting major plazas were laid out on his grid. These are the Gran Via de les Corts Catalanes, or Gran Via, parallel to the sea, and the Passeig de Gràcia, perpendicular to it. A long boulevard, the Avinguda Diagonal (see pp. 82–84), cut across the new district from the coast to the hills. The central points were to be the new Plaça de Catalunya, between the head of the Rambla and the Passeig de Gràcia, and the Plaça d'Espanya and the Plaça de les Glòries Catalanes on the Gran Via between Montjuïc and the Diagonal.

Tearing down the walls was like removing a corset from the old girl. Barcelona could breathe. Construction (and land speculation) went ahead at a fast pace. As they had done in earlier times of transition, the rich and the middling rich moved into the new district and built large homes. The notion of gardens within the blocks was quickly abandoned, land being too valuable. The Passeig de Gràcia, so named because it leads to the village of Gràcia now swallowed up by Barcelona, became the place to be seen. The moment coincided with the 1888 Universal Exposition, Barcelona's open house to show the world its new face, and with a European vogue in design for what the French called Art Nouveau, the Germans called Jugendstil and the Spanish dubbed Modernisme. It was a rebellion against the rigid forms and colourless stone and plaster of the classical architecture that had replaced Gothic. Nowhere did this style thrive and take on nationalist motifs and meaning as in Barcelona, and nowhere has it been so carefully preserved.

Antoni Gaudí and Barcelona have become synonymous for many who have only seen his work in photographs. The eccentric genius lived a long, productive life and his handiwork is found all over the city. But others excelled in the new style too, notably Lluís Domènech i Montaner (1850–1923), creator of the astonishing Palau de la Música Catalana (see pp. 59–60), and Josep Puig i Cadafalch (1867–1957), responsible for the turreted Casa de les Punxes on the Diagonal **53**

Gaudí

No individual has left so personal a mark on a city as Antoni Gaudí on Barcelona. His style is so much his own that he has not been the fount of a continuing school and now seems to have been the only one of his kind. Looking back, one wonders how he convinced conservative merchants and churchmen to accept his far-out ideas. Count Eusebi Güell, a textile manufacturer, was his patient patron.

The Palau Güell, which Gaudí began in 1885, previews many aspects of Gaudi's work, in that it draws on styles of the past—Gothic and Moorish—and distorts them as a dream distorts reality. He was a talented designer of furniture and interior decorations and closely supervised every detail of the assignments he gave his artisans. The Sagrada Família gave scope to these trends and went far beyond them.

For all his innovations, Gaudí was no Bohemian, but deeply religious and conservative in his own lifestyle, too. He had a sense of humour, too. When a client complained that there was no room for her piano in the music room he designed, Gaudí's response was "let her take up the violin". The architect died in 1926, hit by a tram. The hospital did not immediately identify the old man with a white beard, but when they did, the whole city turned out for his funeral.

and Els Quatre Gats, the artists' café at No. 3 Carrer Montsió. Both were prominent in the politics of Catalonia.

Houses of all three are found in one block called the "Block of Discord" on the west side of the Passeig de Gràcia between the Carrer del Consell de Cent and Carrer d'Aragó. (In

Catalan the word for "apple" and "block" are the same—*mançana*—allowing this play on words alluding to the apple in Greek mythology awarded to the most beautiful among three goddesses, a contest that led inevitably to trouble.) The first house, at No. 35, is the **Casa Lleó Morera** (1905), by Domènech i Montaner. It incorporates Moorish and Gothic elements, as well as decorations using recent inventions: the telephone, camera and light

Rooftop fantasy turns chimneys into dragons, a Gaudí hallmark.

bulb. The main floor is now occupied by the Barcelona Tourist Department, so visitors can at least get a peek at the interior, richly decorated with carvings, mosaics and stained glass. In the **Casa Amatller** (1900) at No. 41, Puig i Cadafalch drew inspiration from the Flemish for his stepped roof faced with glazed tiles. The Institut Amatller d'Art Hispànic here has furniture by the architect.

The Gaudí house, the **Casa Batlló** (1904), is next door. It is in an extreme personal style that immediately sets Gaudí apart from the others. The curvy contours, unexpected combinations of textures and materials, bright colours and infinite detail are Gaudí hallmarks. Very often religious or nationalist symbolism is present. The Casa Batlló, for example, is said to symbolize Catalonia's patron, St. George, and the dragon. Gaudí left no clues on the matter. The blue tile roof with orange knobs could be the dragon's scaly back and the window balconies the skulls and bones of its

Learning to dance the sardana *is*
56 *part of growing up in Catalonia.*

victims, while St. George's cross and a shaft suggesting a spear stab down from above. The façade is covered with the bits of broken-plate and tile surfacing he introduced and with blue disks that are like bubbles rising in water.

No. 92, farther up and across the street, is the **Casa Milà**, known as La Pedrera, a Gaudí apartment house of 1905 that is classified by Unesco as an artistic World Heritage Site. Tours of the building are conducted by the Fundació Caixa de Catalunya (apply at the concierge's office for the times). The sinuous façade with wrought-iron balconies that have been likened to seaweed is topped by a cluster of fanciful chimneys of swirling shapes that have mask-like apertures. The roof is a great place for photographers to snap the city with these bizarre forms in the foreground. Note the detail of carved doors (even the doorknobs are handcrafted), cobweb window frames and metal ribbon patterns on bannisters. Gaudí gave the building one of the world's first underground parking garages.

Outside you'll be walking on the pink and turquoise hexagonal tiles he designed for the pavements of the Passeig de Gràcia. The mosaic benches and iron street lamps with little bats (1900) are by Pere Falqués. Executing the intricate designs of the Modernist architects involved batteries of skilled cabinet makers, masons, iron workers and artists in glass and ceramics. You'll find more examples of this unique style by other architects of the period in the streets crossing the Passeig de Gràcia to the east, such as Diputació, Consell de Cent, Mallorca and València over as far as the raucous Mercat de la Concepció market. (In the old town, too, are marvellous Art Nouveau store fronts, such as the Filatèlia Monge stamp shop at Carrer dels Boters 2, and the Antiga Casa Figueras bakery on the Rambla.)

The **Passeig de Gràcia** is a favourite street for strolling. There are outdoor cafés, cinemas, galleries combining many shops in one arcade, bookstores, quality leather goods and fashion boutiques. Some of the top hotels are on or near this avenue, and many travel agencies and airline offices. The **Plaça de Catalunya**, where it begins, was designed to be the city's hub. The bus, metro and regional train systems radiate from this square. Unfortunately it lacks character. It is too big and too empty, despite encircling trees and the usual robust 19th-century statues. Big banks hedge it in and it is a place one hurries across to get to the Rambla or the Passeig de Gràcia or the big department stores. It comes to life when the city stages rock concerts and other events in the central plaza. On Saturdays from 10.30 a.m. to 1.30 p.m. mothers bring their children here for free lessons in dancing the *sardana*. Should you sit down to watch, a man will soon come up to ask a small rental fee for the chair.

An extension of the old Rambla, the **Rambla de Catalunya** also climbs the slope here, parallel with the Passeig de Gràcia. Check the Sala Cultural of the Caja de Ahorros de Madrid savings bank on the corner for announcements of free concerts and lectures. The Rambla de Catalunya has a central walkway between Carrer de la Diputació and the Diagonal. More cinemas, boutiques and bars, more banks, hotels, pastry shops (Mauri at the corner of Carrer de Provença is rather special), and more of the fast food shops that are encroaching on the *tapa* bars in midtown. Two blocks west of this Rambla on the Gran Via is the old university centre at the Plaça de la Universitat.

Palau de la Música Catalana

Gaudí's monuments are the most original, but the most perfect expression of Modernisme is Lluís Domènech i Montaner's Palau de la Música Catalana. This peacock of a building is more decorated than the Tatooed Lady. No surface is left bare of its bit of mosaic, tile, stained glass, enamel, sculpture or carving; no angle of vision is free from the tumultuous assault of contours and colours. To see it properly, one must attend a concert, for it cannot normally be visited otherwise. Tickets may be had during the season, October through June, at the box office (burrowed into a mosaic) on the Carrer Sant Pere més alt near the top of Via Laietana.

The hall was built in 1908 for a musical society called the Orfeó Català. Its programmes always feature top symphony orchestras and soloists. The brick exterior is overpoweringly worked with Moorish arches, columns inlaid with floral designs in tile, stone roses and, swelling over a large mosaic of singers, Montserrat and the Catalan flag, what looks like a giant Easter egg. In the midst of all this, formal busts of **59**

Beethoven & Co. on the façade all look a bit disconcerted.

The exterior is sober compared to what's inside. Once again, every inch is embellished down to the tiles underfoot. The hall is nevertheless light and roomy. There are three tiers of seating and, because the structural skeleton is of iron—an innovation in those days—the walls, not needed for support, are free to be glass. It is stained of course. Sunlight at afternoon concerts supplements the rings of lights hanging at an angle from crown-like chandeliers. On either side of the orchestra's stage the rich colours of the room are offset by two wildly sculpted groups in white plaster: on the left maidens and garlands under a tree that branches over the stage and shelters a large bust of the Catalan folk music composer Josep Anselm Clavé; on the right, Beethoven between two Parthenon pillars through which a wreath of smoke rises to become a brace of plunging horses and shrieking Valkyrie. Between these fevered creations of the sculptor Pau Gargallo, Picasso's friend, the silvery pipes of a grand organ stand in orderly contrast.

Overhead is the Palau's crowning glory, a ceiling of stained glass that is at once a hanging bowl and an orb of golden discs that radiate flames towards segmented rings of angel faces. The level of boxes is open, the chairs enclosed by a curving rail of wood in front of the tall windows. There's no traditional red plush and gilt here, but pastel tones of rose and green and amber. Behind the musicians a curving wall is covered with mosaics of muses playing instruments, from bagpipes to castanets. Magically, the upper part of their bodies is porcelain and seems to emerge from the walls. The whole thing verges on the chaotic, but is nevertheless marvellous.

El Raval

The district between the Rambla and the Ronda de Sant Antoni, once the line of the city wall, is El Raval, a neighbourhood that is being upgraded. The best way to find the historic buildings around here is to start on the Rambla turning west on the Carrer del Carme or walk through the Boqueria market. At the corner of the market's

Revival of the old district around Sant Pau del Camp brings to light vestiges of a more recent past.

parking lot is **Plaça de Doctor Fleming**, the little square dedicated to Sir Alexander Fleming, the discoverer of penicillin. Four cabins here are occupied by public scribes, ready to compose a love letter or fill out official forms, the last practitioners of an ancient trade.

Rejoin the Carrer del Carme here and turn into the Gothic complex of the **Hospital de la Santa Creu** (Hospital of the Holy Cross). A hospital and refuge for pilgrims stood on this spot for a thousand years. Gaudí died here in 1926, shortly before the medical establishment was moved across the Diagonal to new quarters designed by Domènech i Montaner. The present structures were begun in 1401. At the left of the Carrer del Carme entrance stands the **Acadèmia de Medicina**, formerly the College of Surgery, and to the right, the wing for convalescents, now the **Institut d'Estudis Catalans**. Look for the frieze of 16th-century tiles on the life of St. Paul in its entryway. The **Biblioteca de Catalunya** occupies the large vaulted hall on an upper floor where the patients once were housed.

The hospital's courtyard is restful, with benches near orange trees that waft a sweet perfume in spring and are hung with golden fruit in summer. Pigeons wheel overhead and kids play under the arches surrounding the patio. Exhibitions of art and books are held in the various halls off the cloister. A gateway opens onto the Carrer de l'Hospital where the Fair of Sant Ponç on May 11 turns the street into a popular and traditional market of herbs.

One more building on this side of the Rambla that should not be missed is the small church of **Sant Pau del Camp**, off in a corner of its own at the end of the Carrer de Sant Pau, which starts at the Pla de la Boqueria. The simplicity of Sant Pau's Romanesque lines is an agreeable change from the extravagance of Barcelona's Modernisme and the intricacies of Gothic. The church was almost certainly built in the 800s, as the tomb of Wilfred II dated 912 was found here. There is a lovely small cloister with curious, rather Arab-style arches. As the church is usually locked, the best time to see the interior and cloister is on a Sunday morning.

A few steps away is the broad Avinguda del Paral.lel and the funicular station for Montjuïc. From here to the port is a district once known for its nightlife. It is called the "Pigalle of

Barcelona" after the bawdy Paris quarter and has gone downhill like the original. The vaudeville houses still operating, such as the venerable El Molino, seem almost as antique as Sant Pau del Camp.

Waterfront

It is said that Barcelona turned its back on the sea in the 19th century and the city became more focused on its industries. The sea wall where families loved to walk and catch the breeze on stifling summer nights was torn down. Access and even a view of the sea was obstructed by warehouses and railway tracks. Expansion was towards the hills, and La Barceloneta, created in the mid-1700s between the port and the beach, became the district of fishermen and sailors. Nowadays all this is changing and the city is rehabilitating its waterfront for recreation.

Christopher Columbus, atop his 50-metre (164-ft.) **Monument a Colom** at the foot of the Rambla, has his back to the city, though Barcelona's boosters say he's pointing the way from his port to the Americas for the common European market of 1992. The cast-iron pillar was put up for the Univer-

sal Exposition of 1888. You can ride a lift to a viewing platform in the globe beneath the statue and from there look down on the traffic whirling around the Plaça Portal de la Pau and the Passeig de Colom that replaced the sea wall with an avenue leading to the exhibition grounds.

A replica of the **Santa María,** Columbus's own flagship, is berthed nearby. The *Santa María* is only half as long at the waterline as the monument is tall, but it held a crew of 40. Aboard ship you can see the admiral's bunk, a map heavily endorsed by graffiti and so many ropes you'd think the ship was towed to America. Nearby is a fleet of *golondrinas* (swallows) and *gaviotas* (gulls), excursion craft that tour the harbour, a pleasant way to spend a half hour. You'll pass under the aerial cable cars that link Montjuïc with La Barceloneta, and chug by the Royal Yacht Club and the docks of cruise ships and the ferries to Mallorca. Just outside the port are floating platforms where mussels are grown on ropes underwater. Four grandiose buildings flank the plaza: the Port Authority *(Puerto Autónomo de Barcelona),* the naval headquarters *(Comandància de Marina),* the mili-

*Ride the cross-harbour cable car
for thrills and a superb view.*

tary headquarters (*Govern
Militar*) and the customs house
(*Aduana*). A skyscraper, the
Torre Colom, is an unfortunate
64 intrusion on the scene.

Across from the Aduana is
the only medieval shipyard
still in existence, Les Reials
Drassanes, begun in 1255. This
is now the **Museu Marítim**, the
Maritime Museum. The 16
bays of these yards could handle more than 30 galleys at a
time and launched ships that
extended Catalonia's dominion

Galley, *La Reial,* aboard which Don Juan of Austria commanded the fleet that defeated the Turks at the Battle of Lepanto in 1571. Eighty Turkish galleys were sunk and 140 captured during the epic three-hour confrontation in which 30,000 Turks and 7,650 Christians died. The richly decorated red and gold galley is 60 metres (197 ft.) long and was powered by 48 oars, each pulled by three men.

The museum also has a fascinating collection of antique parchment maps, including one that belonged to Amerigo Vespucci. There are carved figureheads, naïvely painted sea chests and primitive *ex voto* paintings made by sailors in thanks for surviving disasters at sea. A model of the wooden *Ictineo,* claimed to be the forerunner of the submarine, is displayed. It was launched in 1859 and was designed to collect coral. Around the corner of the Drassanes is a stretch of the 14th-century third wall with towers.

over the Mediterranean from Tunis to Greece, Sicily, Sardinia and much of the French coast. The museum presents models of these ships and others of the cargo and passenger vessels that made Barcelona their home port up to the present day. The prize exhibit is the full-size copy of the Royal

A first step in upgrading the harbour area was converting the **Moll de Bosch i Alsina** (better known as the Moll de la Fusta, the wood-loading quay) into a broad promenade. Once again Barcelonans can stroll by the sea and take refreshment at the restaurants and bars. A large and convenient parking garage is located underneath.

Several impressive structures line the thoroughfare a little way inland called **Carrer Ample,** which roughly means "Broadway". Indeed, for a time the leaders of Barcelona society had their mansions in this street, as the large carriage entrances and ornamented patios of now-neglected buildings attest. Today, it and the parallel **Carrer de la Mercè** are favourites with students who crowd the smoky bars, stocked with wine barrels and with hams, sausages and strings of garlic hanging from the ceilings.

Carrer Ample begins at the Plaça Duc de Medinaceli, a palm-lined square off the harbourside avenue, and passes the church of **La Mercè**, dedicated to the Mare del Déu de la Mercè, co-patroness of Barcelona with Santa Eulàlia. The Feast of La Mercè, in the last week of September when most of the tourists have gone, is one of the city's most popular celebrations.

The **convent of La Mercè**, now converted into the Capitania General, another military installation, was headquarters of an order created to ransom Catalans captured by Barbary Coast pirates. The great author of *Don Quixote,* Miguel de Cervantes, was such a prisoner and is supposed to have lived for a time at No. 2 Passeig de Colom, where he perhaps wrote the often-quoted praise of Barcelona, "Archive of courtesy, the stranger's refuge, shelter of the poor, home of the brave, avenger of the abused... unique for its site and beauty." The Carrer Ample and the Passeig de Colom end at the Central Post Office.

The most remarkable institution on this stretch of the waterfront is **La Llotja**—which has been a centre of Barcelona's trading instincts for more than 600 years. It started out as an open loggia where merchants and ship owners made their deals. In the late 14th century this was enclosed and expanded to three naves of slim columns supporting high round arches. Here was installed the office of "Consulate of the Sea", the foundation of maritime law for all the Mediterranean countries. With the addition of a

Giant lobster and cool breezes draw crowds to harbourside cafés.

WATERFRONT

Wellington
Wellington
d'Icària
Don Carles
200 m
200 yards
100
100
0

Museu
d'Art Modern
Pg. de Pujades
Museu
de Zoologia
Museu
Martorell
Parc de la Ciutadella
Parc Zoològic
P. de Circumval·lació
Avinguda
Pg. de Picasso
C. de Fontanella
Avinguda
LA BARCELONETA
Passeig Marítim
Museu Picasso
Ribera
del Comerç
Bonn
Estació
Terminal
França
Av. M. de l'Argentera
Pge. la Cadena
Dr. Giné
Carrer passeig picasso
Ginebra
Manufactura
C. de la Princesa
C. de Montcada
Museu Textil
de la Indumentària
Mosques
Sta. Maria
del Mar
Llotja
Via Laietana
Plaça
d'Antoni López
Passeig Nacional
Moll de la Barceloneta
Palau Reial
Pl.
Berenguer
Gran
Sants
Just i
Pastor
Correus
Regomir
Caldera
Catedral
Pl. de
St.
Jaume
d'Avinyó
Palau
Episcopal
Palau
de la
Generalitat
Ajuntament
Palau
Centelles
Esglèsia
de la Mercè
Plaça
del Mercè
Passeig de Colom
Moll de Bosch i Alsina
(Moll de la Fusta)
Carrer de Ferran
Còdols
C. Nou de
St. Francesc
Josep Anselm Clavé
Moll d'Espanya
Santa Maria
del Pi
Plaça
Reial
Museu
de Cera
José Anselmo
Escudellers
N
Carrer de Carme
Hospital
de la Sta. Creu
Sant Pau
Gran Teatre
del Liceu
C. de la Rambla
Palau Güell
Arc del Teatre
La Rambla
Monument
a Colom
Plaça Portal
de la Pau
Aduana
Moll de Barcelona
Estació
Marítima
Les Reials Drassanes
(Museu Marítim)
Avinguda de les Drassanes

neoclassical façade, staircase and upper storeys, the building served variously as a Chamber of Commerce and School of Beaux Arts (Picasso was a student) before becoming the **Barcelona Stock Exchange** *(Borsa de Barcelona)*. You can visit the exchange just after it closes at noon, still filled with hubbub and cigar smoke.

Under the arcades across the Passeig d'Isabel II is the stockbrokers' retreat, the Siete Puertas restaurant. Behind the arcades is a flourishing cut-price shopping area of watches, household appliances and electronic wares. And here the harbour turns and La Barceloneta begins.

▶ La Barceloneta

La Barceloneta is not a "little Barcelona" as the name implies. It is separated from the city as much in spirit as by the physical barriers of water and the soon-to-disappear rail yards. No pompous banks, no mod shops, no hallowed Gothic shrines in this shirt-sleeve community of people who catch fish, cook and serve it, eat and drink hearty and yell back and forth at each other over the noise of radios from balconies overhanging neighbourly streets.

La Barceloneta came into being to replace the Ribera district, demolished to make way for the Ciutadella fortress. A triangle of sand, the area now bordered by the Passeig Nacional along the port, by the Avinguda d'Icària following the railway, and by the beachfront Passeig Marítim, was chosen to house the dispossessed families. The triangle was divided into narrow blocks like boxcars, one apartment wide, so that every room could have windows for air and sun. Here, as in many quarters of Barcelona, the windows are shaded by *persianas,* long blinds that hang over the balcony edge to keep out the glare but let in the breeze. And here, too, pots of flowers bloom overhead and canaries trill cheery solos and answering choruses. Fishermen unload their boats across the Passeig Nacional, and the catch soon finds its way to the scores of bars, taverns and restaurants nearby.

At the end of the harbour, turn in a block or two to the **Platja de Sant Miquel** (St. Michael's Beach) where a row of flimsy wooden restaurants fronts on the sea. Each is touted by a parking attendant who tries to steer you into his establishment. The entry is always **69** through a kitchen where oil hisses and kettles give off clouds of savoury steam. This is the place for that paella you've been waiting for, and for a chilled bottle of straw-coloured *blanc sec* or rosé wine. In summer the tables move farther and farther out onto the beach, which is quite illegal. The city threatens to close these restaurants, especially with the Olympic Village rising next door, creating a modern community as big as La Barceloneta itself. Before leaving you might want to duck into the small aquarium at the end of the promenade.

There is a good bus service to La Barceloneta—take the 17 or the 59 from the Plaça de Catalunya—and a sensational ride back can be had aboard a cabin of the 1,292-metre-long (4,239-ft.) aerial **cable car**. Here the tower is 78 metres high (256 ft.), rising to 107 metres (351 ft.) at the first stop above the harbour, where you can descend and walk back to the Columbus monument area, or continue on to Montjuïc at the level of the amusement park.

Montjuïc

Montjuïc, Barcelona's playground, is the natural site for the Olympic Ring *(Anella Olímpica)* of athletic facilities. For years it has combined the features of a green park, a sports centre, a cultural complex of museums, varied

The Palau Nacional's domes loom
70 *majestically on Montjuïc's flank.*

amusement attractions and a venue of almost continuous trade shows. Its 210-metre (689-ft.) summit is a favourite excursion goal for its panoramic view of the city and harbour. In Roman times a road ran from the Mons Taber citadel to Mons Jovis, the mount of the god Jupiter for whom the hill is believed to be named. Others claim the origin is from Mons Judaicus or "Hill of the Jews", after a Jewish cemetery found on its slopes. From 1992 it will be a new Mount Olympus.

Traditionally, Montjuïc enjoyed two roles, that of a garden where olives and vines were cultivated and windmills

turned in the breeze, and that of a lookout and fortress, where signal fires showed the way to ships at sea and where Spanish guns were pointed at the rebellious Catalan city rather than at any foreign invader. Montjuïc really came into its own as the site of the 1929 International Exhibition. The **Plaça d'Espanya**'s ornate fountain was created to grace the entrance to the fairground. This is still a good point to begin a visit to Montjuïc, as it is a main metro and bus stop. The 1929 fair was a strange mixture of architectural styles. The gateway is marked by two brick columns reminiscent of St. Mark's Campanile in Venice. Then a number of hangar-type halls used during the year by commercial exhibitors at fairs line a central pedestrian avenue leading upwards to the vast

Magic Fountain's jets dance in a ballet of sound and colour.

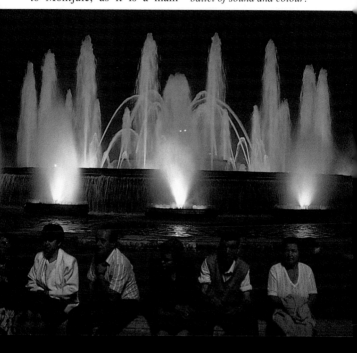

Palau Nacional, the fair's Spanish pavilion. This pompous, leaden pile, domed like the U.S. Capitol, has been redeemed to hold one of the world's finest collections of medieval art, the Museu d'Art de Catalunya (see p. 79–81). The one outstanding building of 1929 was the marble and glass German pavilion designed by Ludwig Mies Van der Rohe. It was taken down after the fair, a mistake rectified in the 1970s, when it was carefully reconstructed as the **Barcelona House**.

In the centre of the fairgrounds is the terrace of the **Font Màgica**, the truly "Magic Fountain". Saturday and Sunday, from 10 p.m. to midnight, the fountains perform a ballet of rising and falling jets bathed in a mist of changing colours set to music. Some 260 combinations are programmed. Couples sit under the trees to listen or wander about with ice-cream cones while the flash bulbs of cameras wink like fireflies. Illuminated fountains rise on both sides of the central avenue down the Plaça d'Espanya, and in your line of sight straight ahead above the city, the lights of Tibidabo shine like an answering beacon. Lit up at night, even the Palau Nacional seems a genuine palace.

Roads winding around the fairgrounds pass other attractions. On the harbour side, off the Carrer de Lleida, is the **Mercat de les Flors**, a former flower market that is now a stage for avant-garde music, theatre and dance. Tickets and information can be had at the Palau de la Virreina on the Rambla. Up the hill and across the street is the **Museu Arqueològic** (Archaeological Museum). Among the many interesting exhibits drawn mainly from prehistoric, Iberian, Greek and Roman sites in Catalonia are reconstructions of tombs and life-like dioramas. Just beyond on the other side of the road is the outdoor **Teatre Grec** (Greek Theatre), built in 1929. In summer, when Barcelona's regular theatres would be uncomfortably warm, the action moves here. Around another curve within walking distance up the hill is the **Museu Etnològic** (Ethnological Museum). This modern and well-presented collection usually has a special programme highlighting the native arts of Latin America and other lands. The Palau de la Virreina will tell you what is currently on display here and the programme of the Greek Theatre.

Farther up Montjuïc and left where the Avinguda de l'Es- **73** tadi, the Olympic Ring boulevard, becomes the Avinguda de Miramar is the simple and elegant **Fundació Joan Miró**. The museum was designed in 1975 by the architect Josep Lluís Sert to receive the paintings, drawings, tapestries and sculpture donated by Miró himself and by contemporary artists and collectors. Josep Lluís Sert, a Barcelonan and friend of Miró, was Dean of the School of Architecture at Harvard University. Miró died in 1983 at the age of 90.

The exhibits follow Miró's artistic development from 1914 onwards. Photographs show him always neatly dressed and barbered, looking like a Catalan businessman in contrast to the Bohemian Picasso, and in contrast, too, with the far-out abstraction he created. The entire collection is witty and bright with the reds, yellows, blues and black always associated with the artist. Note the large *Tapís de la Fundació* tapestry (1979), burly, ropy and powerfully coloured. The *Woman Dreaming of Evasion* (1945), *Morning Star* (1946) and *Claro de Luna* (1968) are among his finest works. Sert's white concrete building is a work of art, too, awarded a special prize in 1977 by the Council of Europe. It is beautifully

and naturally lit by the sun through unseen skylights. A most agreeable garden restaurant in the museum serves a light lunch and refreshments.

The Avinguda de Miramar continues past the station of the funicular railway that climbs the hill from the Avinguda del Paral.lel near the Paral.lel metro stop. The funicular links up here with a cable car that goes to the **Parc d'Atraccions de Montjuïc**, an amusement park, and on to the **Castell de Montjuïc** on the summit. These cars run only on weekends. A short walk from the amusement park is the Plaça de l'Armada station of the aerial cabin that crosses the harbour, completing an interesting network of transport by cable.

The fortress atop Montjuïc was built in 1640 and remained in use by the army and then as a prison until shortly before it was turned over to the city for a museum in 1960. The **Museu Militar** (Military Museum) has an extensive collection of antique weaponry and armour, thousands of lead soldiers of

Woman meets "Woman" at the Fundació Joan Miró museum.

different epochs and models of Catalan castles. Here you'll find in a basement room what may be the only statue of Generalísimo Francisco Franco to be seen in Barcelona today. The fort has sombre associations for the city. Its cannons bombarded the population to put down rebellions in the 18th and 19th centuries and it was the site of political executions, including that of Lluís Companys, President of the Generalitat of Catalonia during the Civil War, shot by a firing squad in 1940.

The far slope of Montjuïc below the fortress is occupied by the **Cementiri del Sud-Ouest**. From the airport road, the tombs look like windows in the mountainside. Many patriots are buried here, some in a common grave, the Fossar de la Pedrera. The present generation has healed the bitter divisions of that cruel war and the dictatorship that followed. It is a subject today's Spain has consigned to history.

The Olympic facilities occupy the northern side of Montjuïc and are centred on the stadium and Plaça d'Europa. The most handsome building is the **Palau d'Esports Sant Jordi**, designed by Japanese architect Arata Izozaki. It can **76** seat 17,000 under a roof 45 metres (147 ft.) high and, after the gymnasts are through with it, will become an indoor stadium and concert hall.

The **Poble Espanyol** (Spanish Village), on Montjuïc's north-eastern flank, is an attraction for which the cliché "fun for the whole family" might have been invented. It's a composite of Spain's varied regions, each represented by replicas of real houses, church towers, fountains, plazas and palaces built of solid brick and stone. The entrance, through one of the gates of the walled city of Avila, is the first step into a community of 115 such reproductions arranged harmoniously along a network of 18 streets and alleys and 11 village squares.

In the Poble Espanyol you can go to the theatre (or park the kiddies in a children's theatre), listen to a band concert or live jazz, see a street festival, do your Christmas shopping (and go to a bank), have an elaborate meal or just a snack of *tapas* in a bar, dance in a discotheque or to an orchestra, see a film or watch a flamenco performance. In a park of more than 4.6 hectares (11.4 acres) there are 13 restaurants, 6 bars, 34 workshops where artisans make regional handicrafts as you watch, and scores of shops

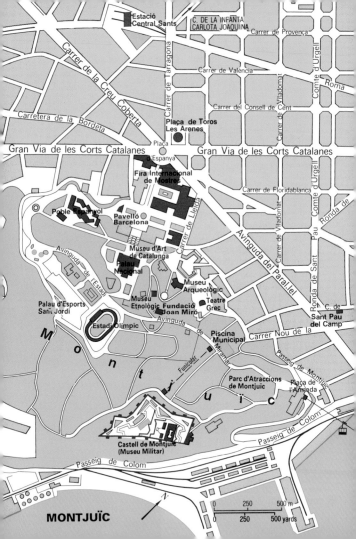

Estació
Central Sants

C. DE LA INFANTA
CARLOTA JOAQUINA

Carrer de Provença

Carrer de la Creu Coberta

Carrer de Tarragona

Carrer de Valencia

Comte d'Urgell

Roma

Carretera de la Bordeta

Carrer del Consell de Cent

Carrer de Villadomat

Plaça de Toros
Les Arenes

Plaça

Gran Via de les Corts Catalanes

Gran Via de les Corts Catalanes

Espanya

Fira Internacional
de Mostres

Carrer de Lleida

Carrer de Floridablanca

Comte d'Urgell

Avinguda del Paral·lel

Ronda de Sant Pau

Ronda de

Poble Espanyol

Pavelló
Barcelona

Avinguda de l'Estadi

Museu d'Art
de Catalunga

Palau
Nacional

Museu
Arqueológic

Museu
Etnológic Fundació
Joan Miró

Teatre
Grec

C. de
Sant Pau
del Camp

Palau d'Esports
Sant Jordi

Estadi Olímpic

Avinguda de

Piscina
Municipal

Carrer Nou de la

M
o
n
t

Funicular

de Miramar

Passeig de Montjuïc

j
u
ï
c

Parc d'Atraccions
de Montjuic

Plaça de
l'Armada

Castell de Montjuïc
(Museu Militar)

Passeig de Colom

Passeig de Colom

N

0   250   500 m

0   250   500 yards

MONTJUÏC

offering these and other typically Spanish products. You can buy castanets, mantillas, Toledo steel blades, dolls, ceramics, leather goods, ropesoled shoes, wines and liqueurs, doll's house furniture and models, religious images, T-shirts—you name it, it's available. The **Museu d'Industrias i Art Popular** (Museum of Traditional Arts and Crafts), where some of these things are being made, is installed in a series of buildings.

One of the most impressive reconstructions is the bell tower in brick and tile of the Aragonese church of Utebo; behind it is the Andalusian quarter, all whitewashed alleys, geraniums, forged-iron grills and lanterns. A 20-minute multi-media show, the **Barcelona Experience**, uses 44 projectors and some 2,500 slides and film clips to cover the city's history and high spots. Cannons boom and heads roll. There's a touching scene of Pau (Pablo) Casals in his 90s speaking at the United Nations and saying "Catalunya was the greatest country in the world".

The Poble Espanyol is fun to visit at night as well as by day. It opens at 9 a.m. The museum and shops close at 8 p.m., but the action in restaurants, cabarets and discos goes on until 2 a.m. (6 a.m. Thursdays to Saturdays). A free double-decker London bus shuttles between the Poble Espanyol and the Plaça d'Espanya until the metro closes at 11 p.m. The at-

Romanesque frescoes are gems of Catalan art museum collection.

traction was built for the 1929 fair, is owned by the city and operated by a private company.

The **Museu d'Art de Catalunya** in the Palau Nacional at the top of the fairgrounds is unmatched in the world for Romanesque art and for Gothic painting of the Catalan school. From the 9th to the 13th centu-ries more than 2,000 churches were built in Catalonia in the Romanesque style of thick, bare walls with rounded arches for doors, windows and cloisters. Interiors were decorated by frescoes in the Byzantine tradition, by primitive sculpture of biblical episodes or rural life on the capitals of columns,

by painted altar front panels and by carved wooden crosses and madonnas of great purity. Around the turn of this century many of these works of art were removed to Catalan museums from churches that were deteriorating or abandoned, thus saving them from further damage or being sold out of the country.

Some of the very best are in this museum, such as the great 12th-century *Christ Pantocrator* from the apse of the church of Sant Climent de Taüll in the Pyrenees. Look for the ingenuous painting of the martyrdom of Saints Quirze and Julita, getting sawed in half, heads stuck with nails and finally, while being boiled in oil, still able to look with calm disdain on their frustrated torturers. A superb group of unpainted, elongated wooden figures representing the descent from the cross is from the church of Santa Maria de Taüll. There are masterpieces in every room of this most unusual collection.

The **Gothic wing** is excellent, too. The first section is arranged with text and photographic enlargements of details that place the scenes, people and symbols in the social and historical context of the feudal period. A lot of the paintings are *retablos*, many-panelled

screens with Gothic-arched frames that stood behind chapel altars. Often the backgrounds show homely furnishings and unaffected glimpses of everyday life that are like snapshots from the past. These paintings, mostly from the 14th to 16th centuries, begin to show the influence of Spain's Flemish and Italian possessions, though they are almost exclusively religious art.

Among the prizes in this wing are Lluís Dalmau's *Virgin of the Councillors*, with its portraits, full of character, of the politicos who commissioned the work for the City Hall chapel in 1445; Jaume Ferrer II's stylishly hatted *St. Jerome*; a curious, very original set of four wooden tomb panels of mourners in striped tubular gowns wildly clutching their flowing red hair and fleeing, as if from some terrible catastrophe; a very fine retable of St. John the Baptist with Saints Sebastian and Nicholas. And just before the exit, look for Ayne Bru's gory throat-slitting of San Cucufate in which the saint's dog is snoozing through the whole nasty business. The ceramics section on an upper floor has examples of Arab sculpture and tiles, including tile scenes of 18th-century life.

The museum is open from

9 a.m. to 2 p.m. every day except Monday. It is currently undergoing extensive remodelling and will be closed for two years. Check with the Palau de la Virreina information office (see p. 30) or the museum itself.

La Ciutadella

On the opposite side of Barcelona from Montjuïc, above the harbour, the cannons of another fort (now converted to a park) once bracketed the city: the infamous Ciutadella, or Citadel. It's a lovely park, too, with a lake, large old trees and pleasant pathways successfully erasing the memory of a grim episode.

When Barcelona surrendered to the troops of King Philip V after a 13-month siege in 1714 (see p. 16), a large fort was constructed on this site to keep the city in line. To make room for La Ciutadella, the fishermen's community of La Ribera was obliterated, including 1,262 houses that were torn down without compensation. To add insult to injury, Barcelona had to pay the costs of building the hated fortress. Although it never saw any military action, it was used as a prison and place of execution. In 1809, as five Catalan patriots were being led to the gallows by French invaders, three Barcelona men tolled the bell of the cathedral. They were hunted down and found under the organ, where they had hidden for 72 hours. Then they, too, were hung on the esplanade of the fort. For Barcelonans, the place became a symbol of oppression, like the Bastille. "Down with La Ciutadella!" was the cry during demonstrations, and great was the joy when it was finally demolished in 1869. This past was exorcized in 1888 when, redesigned as a park, it was the site of the Universal Exposition that celebrated Barcelona's emergence as a modern metropolis.

The **Arc del Triomf** in Moorish-style brickwork was erected as the entrance to the fair at the end of what is now the Plaça Lluís Companys, across the Passeig de Pujades from the park. A statue of Rafael Casanova once stood in this plaza and served as the rallying point for nationalist demonstrations every September 11. This major holiday, the Diada de Catalunya, is the anniversary of the death of Casanova, leader of the city's resistance, who fell here in 1714. All that's left of the original fort are the chapel, governor's palace (now a school) and the arsenal, today **81** divided between the Museu d'Art Modern and the seat of the Parlament de Catalunya. The art collection is in the process of being moved to the Museu d'Art de Catalunya on Montjuïc so that the entire building can be used by the regional parliament.

Despite its name, most of the contents of the **Museu d'Art Modern** seem very dated. There are acres of romantic portraits and landscapes of the 19th century, much of it derivative from the French. There are, however, some notable canvases by Santiago Rusiñol and Ramon Casas, including the amusing painting of the latter on a tandem bicycle with Pere Romeu which hung in the Els Quatre Gats café. This artists' hangout on the Carrer Montsió was where Picasso in 1900 had his first show, sketches of the bar's patrons. There is a Casas charcoal portrait of the young Picasso (1901) and a stone bust of the painter looking like a roughneck, with a cockeyed grin and hair over one eye (1931) by Pau Gargallo. Look for the charming dream-like family group painted by the Russian emigré, Olga Sacharoff. You won't have to search for Mariano Fortuny's *The Battle of Tetuan* (1873). It is so **82** large it takes up almost as much

space as the battle itself. A patio crammed with "materials from diverse sources", hanging, leaning, painted and weathered stalks, might be titled "Gaudí lives!" It is Josep Guinovart i Bertran's abstract happening, *Contorn-Entorn*.

About a third of the park is the **Barcelona Zoo** *(Parc Zoològic)*. It is well laid out under trees, and many enclosures are behind moats, without bars. A star performer is Copito de Nieve (Snowflake), a rare albino gorilla who will sometimes come to the edge of his moat when called by name. There is a show of performing dolphins and a killer whale a number of times daily. Near the marine theatre is a beloved Barcelona **fountain**, the lady with an umbrella whose spokes drip water onto her daintily outstretched hand. The zoo opens daily from 9.30 a.m. to 7 p.m. in summer, and 10 a.m. to 5 p.m. in winter.

The Diagonal

The broad, tree-lined Avinguda Diagonal slices across Cerdà's grid of blocks from the coast to the hills. He designed it for through traffic and it links up with the ring roads around the city and the toll highways beyond. It's largely industrial up to the **Plaça de les Glòries Catalanes**, where a flea market occupies a large space, and becomes increasingly dignified after crossing the Passeig de Sant Joan at the Plaça Mossèn Jacint Verdaguer. Between the Passeig de Gràcia and the Plaça de Francesc Macià it is positively elegant, with four-star hotels and luxury shops. Pricey restaurants and discotheques abound in adjoining streets. This atmosphere holds on the lower side of the avenue. The districts on the hillside were once separate villages, now absorbed by Barcelona's expansion. They still preserve a special character.

Gràcia, for example, has its own town square, the Plaça Rius i Taulet, and streets named Llibertat and Fraternitat and a Plaça Revolució that reflect its radical past. There's a great night-time blowout of food and festivity in these streets in the second half of August. **Horta**, near the site of the Olympic velodrome, is farther out. On its fringes, set in the park of an aristocratic estate, is the amusing Laberint, a 200-year-old maze of yew hedge usually filled with squealing kids and flustered teachers. The atmosphere of **Sarrià** and **Pedralbes** is patrician—villas with gardens and the city's most expensive real estate. The **Monestir de Pedralbes** has a superb Gothic church and a charming two-storeyed cloister. Queen Elisenda de Montcada, who founded the convent in 1326, is buried here, watched over by a community of nuns. Visiting hours are 9.30 a.m. to 2 p.m., except Mondays. Pedralbes can be reached on the regional railway from the Plaça de Catalunya.

After the Plaça de Francesc Macià, the Diagonal is the Barcelona of tomorrow. Here are the most modern office buildings, faculties of the university and the latest hotels. The 120,000-seat stadium of the F.C. Barcelona is between the Diagonal and Montjuïc here. On the other side of the avenue, surrounded by a park, is the **Palau Reial de Pedralbes**, an estate of the Güell family converted into a royal residence in 1924 in case King Alfonso XIII should drop by. It now houses elements of the **Museu de les Artes Decoratives** and a collection of carriages. Renaissance- and Baroque-period paintings from the **Colecció Cambó**, formerly in the Palau de la Virreina, are now hung here. Be sure to go around the park walls to see the dragon gate in wrought iron designed **83** by Gaudí for the Güells. The museum is currently closed for renovation.

🏃 La Sagrada Família

What the Eiffel Tower is to Paris, the statue of Liberty is to New York, or the Parthenon is to Athens, the spires of the Sagrada Família church are to Barcelona. They are the immediately recognizable symbol of the city, their spiky profile visible from afar, like a clump of cypresses, and unmistakable, for there is nothing remotely like them in the world. Few people who have not seen the eight peculiar, cigar-shaped perforated towers realize that they only mark the shell of a cathedral that was begun in 1882 and is still far from completion. Fewer still are aware that if Antoni Gaudí's plans are followed, ten more towers will be added surrounding a 170-metre (558-ft.) central spire as tall as the Washington Monument.

Gaudí died in 1926 at the age of 74 and was buried in the crypt. During his last years he lived in a room inside the construction site, obsessed with the project. A museum in the crypt has models and drawings that show what the finished build-

ing would look like, but Gaudí did not leave detailed plans. During his lifetime he completed the crypt begun by an earlier architect and supervised work on the east Portal of the Nativity, one tower, part of the apse and nave. The west Portal of the Passion and its towers have been under construction by other architects following his style since 1952. The main Portal of the Resurrection on the Carrer de Mallorca has not been started.

The east façade shows best what Gaudí intended. Everything has significance and a name and no space is left unfilled. The three doorways, with stonework dripping like stalactites, represent Faith, Hope and Charity and are loaded with sculpture depicting the birth and youth of Jesus, angel choirs and musicians, the Flight into Egypt, the Slaughter of the Innocents, in the centre the Tree of Calvary, "etcetera, etcetera", as one is forced to continue in describing anything by Gaudí. Seeds and wildflowers found on the site surmount some of the towers and

Gaudí's Sagrada Família's spires are synonymous with Barcelona.

others are upheld at the base by tortoises, or entwined in vines, crawled over by snails and embellished with all kinds of living things. The cathedral is intended to incorporate every aspect of creation and faith. Twelve towers, four at each portal, are to represent the Apostles; four higher ones, the Evangelists; a dome over the apse, the Virgin; and the central spire, the saviour. An elevator and steps give access to a look-out from one of the east towers. On the west side, large letters in orange tile proclaim "Sanctus", and "Hosanna in Excelsis" is executed in "broken-plate" mosaic at the tips.

With all this exuberance, the basic design is still recognizably rooted in Barcelona's Gothic tradition. In the Sagrada Família, Gaudí went beyond the Art Nouveau of his Modernist peers to create something new and highly personal. Whether or not it will ever be finished is a matter of controversy. Funds from private contributions trickle in at a pace that barely keeps the work ticking over. Some critics say the best thing to do now would be to take down the cranes and hoardings, plant grass amid the typically Gaudian tilted columns of the nave and turn it into a park.

Parks

On the rising slope of the hills behind Gràcia, the **Parc Güell** is a compendium of Gaudí's most distinctive devices in a setting of shady paths that overlook the city and the sea. Count Güell bought 6 hectares (15 acres) here, intending to create a community of villas, and in 1900 gave Gaudí carte blanche to produce something original. For the next 14 years, on and off, the architect evidently had fun with the assignment. From the entrance on the Carrer d'Olot, where his gingerbread gatehouse stands beside a forged-iron portal, to the tilted tunnel walkways, dripping with cave-like encrustations, atop the hill, Gaudí's trademarks are omnipresent.

There's the familiar double cross on spires, a dragon, slanted columns, an egg, acres of broken ceramic surfaces (glazed to Gaudí's order and smashed for him), mask-eyes as windows and a Gaudian patchwork of colours and contours. Here is the famous serpentine wall of tile mosaic that serves also as a winding bench around a raised plaza. This space, which regularly inspires impromptu *sardana* dancing, is supported beneath by the **Saló de les Cent Columnes** (Hall of

Tibidabo

The first bright, clear morning of your visit, head for Tibidabo, the 542-metre (1,778-ft.) peak that overlooks Barcelona. A cab can take you to the funicular station, but it is more fun to ride the little blue wooden tram with shiny brass fittings of 1900 vintage. The blue tram stop for Tibidabo may be reached from the Plaça de Catalunya by the train (not metro, though the cars look the same) to "Av. Tibidabo". Be careful not to take the train to "Peu del Funicular", which sounds right, but isn't. The tram takes ten minutes to wind up the Avinguda de Tibidabo to the station, giving you a glimpse of another Barcelona of comfortable villas and gardens. Another five minutes on the funicular lifts you through pine woods to the top and a spectacular panorama of the city, the sea coast and, on very clear days, Mallorca and the Pyrenees' snow crests. A pleasant outdoor café adjoins the funicular station, and at the top there is a restaurant with a terrace.

Tibidabo is a curious mixture of amusement park and religious shrine. The church of the Sagrat Corazon surmounted by a monumental Christ in benediction can be seen from afar, overshadowed by a TV antenna and encircled by the tracks of the amusement park train. Spread before you from the terrace is all Barcelona, with the Prat de Llobregat airport to the right and the spires of the Sagrada Família to the left, and the harbour, the green band of the Rambla, Montjuïc and the Olympic complex straight ahead. *"Haec omnia tibi dabo"* (All this I will give you)—the devil's temptation of Jesus on the mountaintop—is the source of this mountain's rather inscrutable name.

Tibidabo's cool breezes can be very refreshing on a stifling summer evening. Then, crowds of families with children come to scream on the roller coaster, spin in a sedate circle aboard a monoplane marked "1928" and sail towards the stars in the giant ferris wheel. There's an amusing museum of working automatons. From the far side of the heights, the serrated ridge of Montserrat can be seen. All you need for an enjoyable outing is good weather and none of the smog that sometimes collects over the city. A popular postcard sold in Barcelona is simply a sheet of grey with the legend "View of Barcelona from Tibidabo".

the One Hundred Columns). There actually are 86, Doric in style, in what was to have been the colony's covered market. If you look closely at the ceiling, you'll see dolls' heads, bottles, glasses and plates stuck in the mosaics.

As a real estate venture the park failed to attract buyers. Only two villas were built. Gaudí lived for a time in one, with a gold-flecked witch's-hat tower. It contains a small museum of furniture by Gaudí and other memorabilia. The property became a park in 1923. It is open from 10 a.m. to 6 p.m. in winter and 9 a.m. to 8 p.m. from June through September. The 24 bus from the Plaça de Catalunya goes to the park.

The city has created a number of interesting parks for the benefit of otherwise neglected neighbourhoods. The **Parc de l'Espanya Industrial**, for example, converted a factory adjoining the Sants railway station into a lake and waterfalls with contemporary sculpture and a post-modern turreted wall. Miró's giant abstract figure *Woman and Bird* in the **Parc Joan Miró** near the Plaça d'Espanya can be seen from afar.

The **Parc de la Creueta del Coll** has won the praise of art critics for works by Ellsworth Kelly, Roy Liechtenstein and Eduardo Chillida. The park has transformed an abandoned quarry in the working-class Carmelo district. Chillida's striking red concrete claw hangs by cables over a man-made lake.

Excursions

Montserrat

The sandstone reef of Montserrat rises out of the Llobregat plain 62 kilometres (39 mi.) north-west of Barcelona in the very heart of Catalonia. Although the view from its 1,235-metre (4,052-ft.) summit can encompass the Pyrenees and Mallorca, it is more significant that from afar one can see the unmistakable serrated outline that gives Montserrat its name, the "Saw Mountain". Montserrat is not on the road to anywhere, yet all roads in Catalonia symbolically lead to Montserrat, the shrine of Catalan nationhood. The landscape is much like the rocky ridges in cowboy movies where the hero and villain shoot it out between the boulders.

The first hermitages on the mountain were perhaps established to escape the Moorish invasion. One such hermitage, dedicated to St. Mary, was enlarged as a Benedictine monastery in the 11th century. Some one hundred years later it became the repository of **La Moreneta**, the little dark madonna, a small wooden image of a brown-faced Virgin holding the infant Jesus on her lap and the globe in her right hand. Pilgrims, from commoners to kings, have climbed the mountain to worship her ever since. She has a special importance to Catalans as their patron, and like Catalan nationalism, the monastery has been destroyed only to rise again. It was burned to the ground by the Napoleonic soldiers in 1808, abandoned in 1835 when all convents were sequestered by the state and rebuilt only in 1874. During the Spanish Civil War, when anti-clerical feelings were violent among the Republicans in Barcelona, La Moreneta was secretly replaced by a copy, and the original was hidden during the Franco years. When Catalan language and traditions were suppressed, Montserrat's monks continued masses in

Saw-tooth ridge of Montserrat shelters world-famed monastery, the shrine of Catalan nationhood.

Catalan and kept the flame alive.

The site is spectacular, tucked in folds of rock high above the plain. A million pilgrims and tourists visit the monastery each year. On the eve of the saint's day, April 27, the monks hold an all-night vigil attended by a multitude. But almost any day of the week scores of busloads of Catalans disgorge in front of the monastery's complex of museum, souvenir supermarket and cafeteria. Many are on village outings, carrying banners and accompanied by a *cobla* of musicians to play as they dance the *sardana* in the large square before the church. There'll be a fellow playing a flageolet with one hand while beating a little drum tied to his arm with the other. A *cobla* will have reedy oboes and horns, too. Sometimes half a dozen *sardana* circles bob up and down at once, filling the square.

A long queue forms to see La Moreneta. She looks down from a gold and glass case above and to the right of the altar, but the faithful can touch or kiss her right hand through an opening in the protecting shield. She looks much like other madonnas in Barcelona's Museu d'Art de Catalunya— or they resemble her—with a long, slender, pointed nose. At noon, the choir boys of the Escolania, one of the world's oldest music schools founded in the 13th century, fill the basilica with their angelic voices. The massed congregation joins in at the end of the service to sing Montserrat's hymn, the *Virolai,* a thrilling expression of faith here fused with a nationalist fervour.

The spires of rock above the monastery are a favourite goal of climbers. It comes as a shock to realize that those little dots on the bare, perpendicular cliffs are *people!* While watching them, you can have a snack in the open-air market where Montserrat honey and a soft goat yoghurt are served in little cups. The monks distill a sweet liqueur called *Aromas de Montserrat* using herbs found on the mountain. From the monastery there are walks to other hermitages and a funicular to the cave sacred to the legend of the madonna. Statues and plaques line the paths. One portrays Pau (Pablo) Casals playing his cello.

Montserrat can be reached easily from Barcelona by bus from the Plaça d'Espanya regional train station to the Colònia Gomis, where a swaying cable car lifts you from the river to the monastery. Trains from the Plaça de Catalunya station to Monistrol link up with buses there for the monastery. By car, leave Barcelona via the Diagonal and onto the superhighway, Madrid–Tarragona direction, exiting at Sortida 25.

Sitges

It's easy to get to the Costa Dorada beaches from Barcelona. The coast south of the city earned its name from its broad, golden sands, in contrast to the rocky coves and piney inlets of the Costa Brava to the north. The goal of a day's outing should be Sitges, the favourite resort of the Barcelonans themselves. Most of the 43-kilometre (27-mi.) drive is uninspiring, passing through endless construction sites and lots of truck traffic until you get to **Castelldefels**. This is still within commuting distance of the city, less than half an hour by train. There's a substantial castle a bit inland, more impressive from a distance than close up.

The coast drive is a scenic but narrow and curvy route that after another half-hour brings **Sitges** into view. Happily the town has escaped the high-rises and tawdry atmosphere of many coastal resorts and retains both beauty and dignity, albeit somewhat overwhelmed by crowds in summer. There are two beaches, separated by a promontory where gleaming whitewashed houses cluster around the church of Sant Bartomeu. The **Museu d'El Cau Ferrat** is installed in the house of the painter Santiago Rusiñol (1861–1931), whose collection of works by El Greco, Ramon Casas, Picasso and others is on display, along with many of his own canvases, ceramics and forged-iron pieces.

Across the street, the **Museu Mar i Cel** (Sea and Sky Museum) holds a small collection of medieval sculpture and paintings in a splendid house overlooking the sea.

La Ribera, the nearest beach, is almost 3 kilometres (2 mi.) long, backed by a promenade lined with cafés and restaurants. The streets are carpeted with flowers for the procession of Corpus Christi in late spring.

On the hillsides and lanes are the half-hidden villas of well-to-do Barcelona families, while the streets between the beach and railway station are geared to food and frolic. There's one more curiosity, the **Museu Romantica**'s large family of antique dolls.

What to Do

Sport

Barcelona's successful bid for the '92 Olympic Games was its third try this century. The city is crazy about sports. To support the present and previous Olympic candidacies, it developed a superb network of playing fields, tracks, courts, pools and riding rings. The visitor won't have any difficulty keeping in shape here, whether by joining the local joggers in the streets and in the parks of Montjuïc, swimming at a beach or enjoying almost any sport. Even skiing in the Pyrenees is only a few hours away.

At the Reial Club de Golf El Prat near the airport, 27 holes provide three different circuits. Clubs and carts may be rented and there's a pool. The Club de Golf Vallromanes is only 23 kilometres (14 mi.) from the city, and the Terramar course near Sitges is about an hour's drive away. Other nearby courses are at Sant Cugat, off the A-7 motorway, and the nine-hole course at Sant Andreu de Llavaneres on the A-19 towards Mataró.

Tennis courts open to the public are located in Pedralbes in the Can Caralleu sports centre, where there are also indoor and outdoor swimming pools. The courts are open from 8 a.m. to 11 p.m. For information on courts, phone 203-7874. Your hotel may also be able to arrange guest privileges at a Barcelona tennis club. Squash courts are available at Squash Barcelona, Av. Dr. del Marañón 17, tel. 334-0258. Riding can be arranged through the Club Hípic de Barcelona. Ciutat de Balaguer 68, tel. 417-3039. For sailing information contact the Reial Club Marítim de Barcelona, tel. 315-0007.

Skiing may be the fastest growing sport in Catalonia. Each year brings new developments in the Pyrenees, most within a few hours of Barcelona: Núria, at 1,963 metres (6,440 ft.); La Molina, whose slopes rise to 2,537 metres (8,324 ft.); and Vallter with 12 slopes and a top station at 2,500 metres (8,203 ft.). Information on the conditions of roads and slopes can be obtained by phoning the Associació Catalana d'Estacions d'Esquí, tel. (93) 238-3135

The great spectator sport in Barcelona is football, and football means team of the Barça. The top-ranked team of the F.C. Barcelona has a 120,000-seat stadium, Camp Nou, in the university district. Consult a newspaper or the nearest local for dates and times of games.

La Corrida de Toros, the bullfight, has never held the place in Catalonia that it enjoys in the south of Spain. One of the city's two bull rings is being replaced by a hotel for the Olympic Games; the other, the Plaza de Toros Monumental on the Gran Via at Passeig de Carles I, usually has something going on Sunday afternoons at 5.30 p.m. from spring through autumn. The cartel, or programme, is often filled by *novilleros*, young apprentices who fight smaller bulls while working their way up to become *matadores*. But any bullfight is a gamble (except for the bull, who always loses). For the *torero*, re-enacting the age-old drama that pits one man's courage and grace against the dark violence of a huge bull, it is a gamble with death or a serious goring; for the spectator it is a gamble against high odds on seeing a really classic *corrida*. True aficionados are routinely disappointed. They are also in the minority in the stands, where the *oles* are cried in English, German, Italian and Japanese accents. But it is well worth going to the Monumental if you've never seen a bullfight. They may not be the best, but they are authentic.

Shopping

You'll find in Barcelona, handicrafts from every corner of the country—those little treasures of hand-wrought iron, pottery, leather and clothing that people like to bring back from Spain. As a city of style and taste, it also abounds in fashion boutiques, antique shops and art galleries. Just remember that, with the exception of the big department stores, most shops are closed between 1.30 and 4.30 p.m. and stay open until as late as 8 p.m. or more.

Behind the cathedral is the place for ceramics, both the traditional tiles, plates, pitchers and bowls in white glaze with blue and yellow decoration, and modern creations. You can browse for hours in the antique shops in narrow streets of the Barri Gòtic, such as the Carrer dels Banys Nous. Many of the offerings are frankly copies, but good copies and sold as such. You'll find copper vessels, chests, old tiles, swords, old medical instruments, clocks, furniture. More of this on a knicknack level is spread out on the stands of dealers at the fair held on Thursdays in the Plaça Nova.

The Passeig de Gràcia, the fashionable streets leading off it in the direction of the Rambla **93**

Pastry shop's Art Nouveau decor is a delightful confection too.

de Catalunya, and also the Diagonal in this area are good hunting grounds for men's and women's fashions. Leather jackets and skirts are good value. The latest vogue is to bring together a dozen or so arcades or a gallery that burrows into a block and winds around inside in a blaze of light and music, like El Boulevard Rosa and the Galerías Halley on the Passeig de Gràcia. El Boulevard dels Antiquaris at 57 Passeig de Gràcia does the same thing for antiques, with 73 shops under one roof.

Down the Rambla you'll find good bookstores and variety shops that sell bullfight posters with your name on them; the leather (or plastic) wineskin called a *bota* and its glass relative, the *porrón;* imitation Toledo steel with the engraving painted on; imitation duelling pistols; and authentically tawdry sex shop trinkets. There are leather factories off the Rambla de Santa Mónica on the Carrer Ample.

A complete selection of better-quality handicrafts and curios can be found in the Poble Espanyol on Montjuïc. One-stop shopping can also be done in the big department stores, El Corte Inglés on the Plaça de Catalunya and the Galerías Preciados nearby in the Portal de l'Àngel. If your purchases are substantial it will be worthwhile to fill out the forms in the shop that will entitle you to a refund of the IVA tax (anything from 6 to 33 per cent depending on the type of goods), mailed to your home address. You must show your purchases to the customs inspector on departure and give him the forms.

Barcelona's flea market, Els Encants, is a totally promiscuous grab-bag of second-hand everything that stretches northwards from the Plaça de les Glòries Catalanes. It is open Monday, Wednesday, Friday and Saturday. If your thing is stamps and coins, go to the Plaça Reial on Sunday morning, or to the Sant Antoni market, where books and records are sold too.

Nightlife

Even when the sun goes down, Barcelona shines. It's a swinging city with every kind of nightlife diversion. In good weather, which is most of the time, the streets at night are slow-moving rivers of strollers. The main churches and monuments are illuminated, taking on a new and graceful aspect. The interior light shining through the stained-glass windows of the cathedral and the lamplight of narrow lanes in the Barri Gòtic bring out details that you miss by day.

The city authorities subsidize concerts, from rock to classical, in the Plaça de Catalunya and in neighbourhood parks. The world's great singers appear in opera at the Gran Teatre del Liceu, while the latest in modern dance, music and experimental theatre is regularly staged in the evenings at the Mercat de les Flors, the old flower market a short walk from the spectacular sound and light show of the Font Màgica (see p. 73). (see p. 73)

The young crowd flock to "design bars" for an after-work drink or an evening of disco dancing. A design bar is an ultra-modern environment. For example, entering Nick Havana, one of the pioneers of the genre, is like emerging into a small square. The bar is divided in sections, each surrounded by café-style tables to form different centres for groups. The disco area with multi-vision images flashing on one wall is separated by a glass panel from a sound-proofed conversation area. There's a corner where a vending machine sells books, and news bulletins are projected on a screen. Another night spot near the broadcasting studios on the Diagonal has a small TV screen on every table of its restaurant. Each design bar has its own theme.

Off the lower Rambla and the Plaça Reial are clubs where flamenco singing and dancing are featured. Several large clubs with orchestras, dancing, elaborate floorshows and restaurants are on the various "Barcelona by Night" tours that can be arranged through hotels. All these attractions can also be found in one place, the Poble Espanyol. In its alleys and plazas are jazz clubs, flamenco artists, big band dancing and discos going strong until 4 a.m.

Festivals

Barcelonans work hard and play hard. Throughout the year, religious and secular holidays turn the different neighbourhoods or the whole city into a carnival. Food, fireworks, music, costumes and especially the tall papier-mâché effigies called *gigantes* and their comical companions, the *cabezudo* walking heads, are essential fiesta features. Each neighbourhood has its own identifying models. The *gigantes* are about 4 metres (13 ft.) high and are elaborately dressed as kings and queens, knights, ladies, gentlemen and country folk. They are carried in stately procession by men concealed under costumes. The *cabezudos,* worn by youngsters or small adults, are usually oversize cartoon heads of well-known personalities or types. They prance about mischievously, accosting people in the crowd.

During many of these festivals, men and boys called *Castellers* climb on each oth-

Every neighbourhood fiesta has its own gigantes, *bobbing and spinning on strong shoulders.*

er's shoulders to form human towers five or six men high in the Plaça de Sant Jaume. The topmost is a small boy who scampers like a monkey to reach up to the balcony of the Ajuntament city hall. Then the tower collapses gently from the top down.

With luck, one festival or another will be going on while you are in Barcelona. Following are the dates of the major events:

January 6	*Día de Reyes* (Three Kings Day), gift giving and pyrotechnical displays.
February	Feast of Santa Eulàlia, parades of *gigantes* , medieval dances.
March/April	Carnival at beginning of Lenten season. Holy Week *(Semana Santa)* with series of religious festivals starting with Palm Sunday procession through Rambla de Catalunya.
April 23	Feast of Sant Jordi, impromptu book stalls are set up and couples exchange flowers.
April 27	Feast of Virgin of Montserrat, liturgical acts, choir singing and *sardana* dancing.
May	Corpus Christi, carpets of flowers and processions in Sitges, also the curious tradition of a "dancing egg" balanced on the spray of the cathedral fountain.
May 11	Feast of Sant Ponç, herb fair in Carrer de l'Hospital.
June 23–24	Feast of Sant Joan, big blowout with fireworks and feasting.
End June-July	*Grec* festival of theatre, classical music, pop and rock.
August 15	Local block parties in the festooned streets of Gràcia in week leading up to Assumption.
September 11	*Diada,* Catalan national day, demonstrations and flag waving.
September 24	A whole week of celebrations to mark Barcelona's main festival in honour of the city's patron, Mare de Déu de la Mercé (Our Lady of Mercy). The Rambla becomes an outdoor banquet hall, the squares bandstands and the streets dancefloors.
December	Fairs for Christmas crib figurines.

Eating Out

All great chefs agree that ingredients make or break a cuisine. And anyone who has walked through one of Barcelona's great covered markets knows that the ingredients here are superb. As a Mediterranean port, just-caught local fish and seafood take pride of place. Fruit and vegetables, known throughout Europe as imports from Spain, here are at their freshest. Mountain-cured hams and spicy sausages, spit-roasted meat and fowl with aromatic herbs and umpteen kinds of omelettes are specialities. Barcelona's cosmopolitan population means you'll find restaurants featuring the food of every Spanish region (Basque cookery is especially appreciated) and from the rest of the world as well.

Where to Eat

Barcelona restaurants run the full range from super-elegant to home-cooking. A grading system from five forks to one, marked on the door of the restaurant, is supposed to announce the category, though the signs are not always prominently displayed. The system is an indication of price and grades the elaborateness of the facilities and service, not the quality of the food. Look for the *menú del día* for the best bargain.

You can eat very well indeed never setting foot in a restaurant. The not-so-little snacks called *tapas* for which Barcelona bars and cafés are world famous come in dozens of delicious preparations, from appetizers, such as olives and salted almonds, through vegetable salads to fried squid, chilled shrimp, lobster mayonnaise, sausage slices, meatballs, spiced potatoes, cheese—almost anything the human frame requires to stave off hunger. The small plates are called a *porción*. A large serving is a *ración*, and half of this is a *media-ración*. You can easily get carried away into spending more on *tapas* than on a complete restaurant meal. But you can also eat *tapas* whenever you want, whereas restaurants serve lunch from about 1 to 3.30 p.m. and dinner from about 8.30 to 11 p.m.

What to Eat

Although it originates in rice-growing Valencia, the classic seafood paella (pronounced pie-ALE-ya) is probably high on every visitor's list of dishes to sample in Barcelona. Paellas can be made with chicken, sausage, rabbit or whatever is **99** handy, piled up on a bed of saffron-tinted rice. The name is taken from the two-handled iron pan it's cooked in. But go to the beach at La Barceloneta and try a paella of mussels, clams, shrimp and several kinds of fish. It will take about 20 minutes to prepare, so your waiter will suggest a "little something" to nibble on while waiting. Then you'll get a platter of deep-fried *pescaditos* (whitebait) and another of little crisply fried *calamares* (squid) caught off the beach. If you choose a *paella parellada,* the shells and bones will have been removed in the kitchen.

A popular local fish served in many ways is *rape,* angler fish, tasty *a l'all cremat,* with creamed garlic. Other good bets are *mero al forn,* baked sea bass, and *llenguado a la graella* or *a la planxa,* a grilled sole. You might be fooled by *truita,* which means both trout and *tortilla,* the Spanish omelette. In spring, *truita d'espàrrecs i alls tendres* is a delicious omelette of asparagus and young garlic. *Bacallà,* the lowly salt cod, is now served in the most distinguished restaurants in various transformations. Typically Catalan are *bacallà amb samfaina,* in a sauce resembling ratatouille, with onions, aubergine, tomato, courgettes

and peppers, and *esqueixada* (pronounced es-kay-SHA-da), which presents the cod shredded in a tart salad of beans, pickled onions, olives and tomato. A *sarsuela* is a stew of fish cooked in its own juices; a *graellada de peix* is a mixed grill of fish. Popular as a bar snack are *berberechos,* cockles. *Anxoves,* anchovies, find their way into many dishes.

A standard starter is the *pa amb tomàquet,* a solid slice of rough textured bread rubbed with the cut half of a fresh tomato and sprinkled with salt and pepper and a trickle of good olive oil. It can also be toasted or rubbed with onion or garlic. Other specialities to try are *llebre estofada amb xocolata,* stewed hare in a bitter chocolate sauce. There's a lobster version of this too. Barcelona's all-purpose sausage is the hearty *botifarra,* often served with *faves a la catalana,* broad beans stewed in an earthenware casserole. The *xató* (pronounced sha-TO) endive and olives salad of Sitges is fortified with tuna (tunny) or cod, and has an especially good sauce made of red pepper, anchovies, garlic and almonds ground to a paste with olive oil and vinegar. The word for salad of any kind is *amanida.* *Escalivada* is an aubergine,

The ambiance of a Barcelona restaurant is as flavourful as the food.

onion and pepper salad. In *espinacs a la catalana,* spinach is mixed with *panses* (raisins) and pine nuts. Lots of mushrooms are found in the hills of Catalonia and the Pyrenees. Look for *moixernons* and the big, meaty *rovellons.*

When it comes to dessert, there'll always be the Spanish custard, *flan,* and the more liquid *crema catalana. Mel i mato* is a honey and creamy cheese treat. But the greatest sweets are those served in the ubiquitous pastry shops.

Drinks

Spanish wines are excellent. The best wines of the Rioja region in Navarre rank with very good Bordeaux, and justifiably cost as much, too. Every restaurant and bar has a house wine, usually from the Priorat or Penedés vineyards of Catalonia. This is what you'll get if you just say *tinto* (red) or *blanco* (white) as most diners do when asked for their choice of *vino.* You'll notice many of them pouring a bit of bubbly mineral water into the wine. This can smooth out a heavy or harsh wine.

Catalonia's sparkling *cava* is excellent and often sold to **101** accompany a luscious dessert in pastry shops. Vintners learned how to make it from the French wineries they supplied with cork. Spanish dark beer on draft is first rate, too. All sorts of spirits are widely available. Because many well-known brands are bottled under licence in Spain, they can be surprisingly cheap.

A popular non-alcoholic drink is *horchata de chufa*. This milky refresher has an almondy taste and is made from a sweet nut. *Horchaterías* are street bars that specialize in this cold drink and in ice-creams.

Barcelona's Bars

The bar in Barcelona is much more than a saloon. It's an institution: restaurant, club, breakfast spot, place of entertainment, and ring-side seat on the passing parade. In its most recent manifestation, the "design bar" (see p. 96), it serves as an architect's showcase. Every block in downtown Barcelona seems to have three or four bars. Some streets, along the Rambla and the port area, have one bar after another.

Typically, a bar has a counter with stools, plenty of standing room and a wide open doorway so that passersby can see what's being offered inside. This will include an array of the hearty snacks called *tapas,* a row of dishes containing at a minimum, anchovies, olives, shrimp, sardines, squid, potato salad, cured ham, salted almonds and a cold omelette filled with sliced potatoes *(tortilla)*. Often bars will list their *tapas* on a blackboard on the sidewalk; a menu of 50 items is not unusual. The microwave oven has made even small bars capable of dishing up hot *tapas.*

The bar will serve coffee black *(solo),* with a spot of milk *(cortado),* or half hot milk *(con leche),* a glass of draught beer *(caña),* soft drinks, red and white wine by the glass, Spanish brandy *(copa)* and popular liqueurs, such as anis. Whiskies and gin drinks may be made with well-known brands produced under licence in Spain. Ask for a martini and you'll get a glass of vermouth. Some bars specialize in the local bubbly *(cava),* sold by the glass.

Barcelonans head for their local bars at mid-morning for a second breakfast, return for a luncheon spread of *tapas,* pop back again during the late afternoon and then after work to meet friends for a drink. When there's a football game on TV the bar will be crowded until the last whistle. Bars have their regulars, of course, and a *tertulia* is an informal group that gathers to discuss a special subject—art, football or whatever.

To Help You Order...

Could we have a table?
Do you have a set menu?

I'd like a/an/some...

beer	una cerveza	milk	leche
bread	pan	mineral water	agua mineral
coffee	un café	napkin	una servilleta
cutlery	los cubiertos	potatoes	patatas
dessert	un postre	rice	arroz
fish	pescado	salad	una ensalada
fruit	fruta	sandwich	un bocadillo
glass	un vaso	sugar	azúcar
ice-cream	un helado	tea	un té
meat	carne	(iced) water	agua (fresca)
menu	la carta	wine	vino

¿Nos puede dar una mesa?
¿Tiene un menú del día?

Quisiera...

...and Read the Menu

aceitunas	olives	judías	beans
albóndigas	meat balls	langosta	spiny lobster
almejas	baby clams	langostino	large prawn
atún	tunny (tuna)	lomo	loin
bacalao	codfish	mariscos	shellfish
besugo	sea bream	mejillones	mussels
boquerones	fresh anchovies	melocotón	peach
calamares	squid	merluza	hake
callos	tripe	ostras	oysters
cangrejo	crab	pastel	cake
caracoles	snails	pimiento	green pepper
cerdo	pork	pollo	chicken
champiñones	mushrooms	pulpitos	baby octopus
chorizo	a spicy pork sausage	queso	cheese
		salchichón	salami
chuleta	chops	salmonete	red mullet
cocido	stew	salsa	sauce
cordero	lamb	ternera	veal
entremeses	hors-d'œuvre	tortilla	omelet
gambas	prawns	trucha	trout
jamón	ham	uvas	grapes
		verduras	vegetables

103

Blueprint for a Perfect Trip

How to Get There

If the choice of ways to go is bewildering, the complexity of fares and regulations can be downright stupefying. Consult a reliable travel agent for up-to-date information on the latest prices and timetables.

BY AIR

There are direct flights to Barcelona from most European capitals and major cities, as well as from various points in North America and North

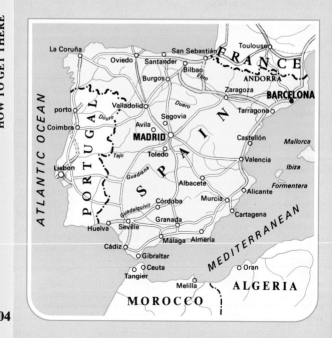

Africa. Flying times: London, about two hours; New York approximately eight hours. Iberia, the Spanish national airline, covers most countries in shared arrangements with their own carriers. A regular shuttle connects Barcelona and Madrid. Consult your travel agent for the schedule of special flights, charters and package deals on offer, such as Iberia's "Barcelona Stop" which allows a free 24-hour stopover in Barcelona, hotel and dinner with entertainment included, on most of their itineraries.

BY ROAD

Drivers heading towards the Mediterranean on the French superhighway network cross into Spain south of Perpignan and join the Spanish *autopista* A-7 (toll motorway) at the frontier post of La Jonquera 150 kilometres (93 mi.) north of Barcelona. An alternative route from Toulouse over the Pyrenees enters Spain at Puigcerdà and follows the N-152 169 kilometres (105 mi.) to Barcelona. The narrow, twisting coast road from the Port Bou border post provides lovely views of the Costa Brava.

Regular coach services also operate from major European cities to Spain and are very comfortable and fast. During the summer many special services are offered with package deals.

BY RAIL

Passengers generally have to change trains at the Spanish frontier, as the Spanish tracks are of a wider gauge than the French. Exceptions are the luxury high-speed Talgo and the Trans-Europ-Express, which have adjustable axles. Significant discounts are applicable to Eurail Pass, Youth Pass and Inter-Rail holders.

BY SEA

For British travellers visiting Barcelona, a ferry links Plymouth and Santander in northern Spain (a 24-hour trip). From Santander, follow the N-240 to Barcelona.

When to Go

Barcelona's mild Mediterranean climate assures sunshine most of the year and makes freezing temperatures rare even in the depths of winter, December through March. Spring and autumn are the most agreeable seasons. Mid-summer can be hot and humid. At times a thick smog hangs over the city. (For temperature chart, see p. 108.)

Planning Your Budget

To give you an idea of what to expect, here's a list of average prices in Spanish pesetas. However, they must be regarded as approximate and vulnerable to inflation.

Airport transfer. Train to city centre 175 ptas.

Baby-sitters. 500 ptas. per hour and up.

Car hire. *Seat Marbella* 2,800 ptas. per day, 24 ptas. per km., 36,400 ptas. per week with unlimited mileage. *Ford Escort* 4,900 ptas. per day, 35 ptas. per km., 56,000 ptas. per week with unlimited mileage. *Renault 21* 8,100 ptas. per day, 58 ptas. per km., 98,700 ptas. per week with unlimited mileage. These prices include unlimited public liability, bail bond and fire and theft insurance.

Cigarettes. Spanish brands 60–180 ptas. per packet of 20; imported brands 195–200 ptas.

Entertainment. Cinema 550 ptas. and 300 ptas. on Wednesdays at certain locations. Theatres 700–2,220 ptas., with special midweek rates. Flamenco nightclub 2,500–3,000 ptas. including one drink, 4,500–5,000 ptas. with dinner. Discotheque 600–1,500 ptas. with one drink. Poble Espanyol 500 ptas., children free (up to 14 years).

Hairdressers. *Woman's* shampoo and set or blow-dry 1,200–2,000 ptas. *Man's* haircut 1,000–1,800 ptas.

Hotels (double room with bath per night). ***** 24,000–44,000 ptas., **** 15,000–25,000, *** 10,000–19,000 ptas., ** 8,000 ptas., * 4,000 ptas. Add 12% IVA for luxury hotels, 6% for other hotels.

Meals and drinks. Continental breakfast 500–1,000 ptas., three-course menu 600–1,500 ptas. including wine; lunch/dinner in a good restaurant 2,000–4,000 ptas.; beer 100 ptas., coffee 90–125 ptas., Spanish brandy 300 ptas., soft drink 100–160 ptas.

Metro or bus. 75 ptas., 80 ptas. on Sundays and holidays and daily after 10 p.m.

Shopping bag. 500 g. bread 80 ptas., 250 g. of butter 250 ptas., dozen eggs 200 ptas., 1 kg. veal 1,300–1,800 ptas., 250 g. of coffee 225 ptas., 1 l. of milk 110 ptas., bottle of wine from 200 ptas.

Taxi. Initial charge 210 ptas. for first 2 km. or six minutes, weekdays between 6 a.m. and 10 p.m 55 ptas. per km. in the city; Saturdays, Sundays and holidays 75 ptas. per km.; 50 ptas. per piece of luggage. There is á 200 ptas. charge for entering or leaving the airport and a 55 ptas. charge at the Sants railway station.

An A–Z Summary of Practical Information and Facts

> Listed after some basic entries is the appropriate Spanish translation, usually in the singular, plus a number of phrases that should help you when seeking assistance.

ACCOMMODATION *(hotel; alojamiento)*. The needs of the Olympic games set off a much-needed hotel building boom in Barcelona. Even so, lodging in the best hotels is often hard to come by and advance reservations are strongly recommended. Spanish hostelries are graded by a star system, with five stars at the luxurious top. About two-thirds of the city's hotels fall in the four- and three-star categories. These classifications often seem arbitrary, with some two- and three-star places fully as good as others rated higher. Since hotel prices were freed from controls, charges have continued to rise and breakfast is rarely included in the room rate. Five- and four-star hotels are subject to 12 per cent IVA tax, lower categories, 6 per cent.

For economy budgets, there are several hundred star-rated guest houses *(hostal, pensión)* and youth hostels *(albergue de juventud)*.

A list of all categories of accommodation may be obtained from the Spanish Tourist Offices in major capitals and cities and on arrival in Barcelona at tourist desks at the airport, railway station and on the Moll de la Fusta quay across from the Columbus monument at the foot of the Rambla.

If possible, select a hotel not too far from the Plaça de Catalunya, a central point convenient for sightseeing and shopping on foot or by public transport.

I'd like...	**Quisiera...**
a double/single room	**una habitación doble/sencilla**
with/without bath/shower	**con/sin baño/ducha**
What's the rate per night?	**¿Cuál es el precio por noche?**

AIRPORT *(aeropuerto)*. Barcelona's airport at El Prat de Llobregat about 15 kilometres (10 mi.) from the city centre will be in the throes of expansion at least until early in 1992.

Buses and trains connect with the city every 20 minutes and take about 20 minutes. The train station is a bit far for passengers with heavy

A luggage, despite escalators and moving walkways, and arriving from the city you are unlikely to find the free baggage trolleys on the platform. Porters are available and there are plenty of taxis.

Banks are open until 11 p.m., tourist information and hotel reservation until about 8 p.m. (3 p.m. on Sundays), and car-hire desks until midnight.

C **CAR HIRE** (*coches de alquiler*). The main international car-hire agencies have offices in Barcelona, and there are reputable Spanish agencies as well. Rates vary considerably so that it is worthwhile shopping around on arrival at the airport or, better still, before you go, when special package deals are often the cheapest. To rent a car, drivers must be over 21 years old and have a valid licence held for at least one year. Third-party insurance is automatically included, but taking out additional full collision coverage is advisable.

I'd like to rent a car (tomorrow).	**Quisiera alquilar un coche (para mañana).**
for one day/a week	**por un día/una semana**
Please include full insurance cover.	**Haga el favor de incluir el seguro a todo riesgo.**

CIGARETTES, CIGARS, TOBACCO (*cigarrillos, puros, tabaco*). Tobacco is a state monopoly, sold in well-marked shops and also in coin machines and by street vendors. Imported cigarettes are expensive. Canary Islands cigars are Spain's best. Havanas are widely available too.

CLIMATE and CLOTHING. From November through April you'll be wise to have a warm jacket or sweater and raincoat. The rest of the year, light summer clothing is in order. Men are expected to wear a jacket and tie in the better restaurants, nightclubs and the opera (where the older Barcelonans like to wear a dinner jacket or long dress and their children wear jeans).

		J	F	M	A	M	J	J	A	S	O	N	D
average daily maximum*	°F	55	57	60	65	71	78	82	82	77	69	62	56
	°C	13	14	16	18	21	25	28	28	25	21	16	13
average daily minimum*	°F	43	45	48	52	57	65	69	69	66	58	51	46
	°C	6	7	9	11	14	18	21	21	19	15	11	8

* Minimum temperatures are measured just before sunrise, maximum temperatures in the afternoon.

COMMUNICATIONS. Main post offices provide facilities for sending telexes and telefaxes as well as a 24-hour telegram service. You can't usually make telephone calls from post offices *(correos)*. The main Barcelona post office is in the port area at Plaça d'Antonio López. Hours are 9 a.m. to 9 p.m. weekdays and from 9 a.m. to 2 p.m. on Saturdays. Smaller branches are only open from 9 a.m. to 2 p.m. weekdays.

Mail. The general delivery or poste restante address in Barcelona is Lista de Correos, Plaça d'Antonio López, Barcelona 08003. The window is in the entry hall of the main post office. You'll need your passport or other identification and must pay a small charge for each letter received. Stamps are also sold in tobacco shops and are usually available in hotels.

Telegrams *(telegrama)*. The telegram office is open from 8 a.m. to midnight weekdays and from 8 a.m. to 10 p.m. Saturday, Sunday and holidays. Telegrams may be sent over the phone 24 hours a day by calling 322 20 00. International operators are linguists, but if you have a language problem, ask your hotel to call in your telegram.

Telephone *(teléfono)*. If you expect to make any international calls, find out how much extra your hotel charges above the regular rates listed in the front of the telephone directory. This may spare you an unpleasant surprise on your hotel bill. You can phone anywhere in the world from the phone booths in the street, and if you have looked up the rates in advance, you can calculate how much change you are going to need. Pick up the receiver and when you get the dial tone, dial 07; wait for a second dial tone to enter the country code, local code and the number you are calling.

To reverse charges, you have to use an operator-manned kiosk (found at airports, seaside resorts, and at the Plaça de Catalunya central telephone exchange). To place a call to Europe and North Africa dial 008; for the rest of the world 005; within Spain 009.

Can you get me this number in...?	**¿Puede comunicarme con este número en...?**
Have you received any mail for...?	**¿Ha recibido correo para...?**
A stamp for this letter/postcard please.	**Por favor, un sello para esta carta/tarjeta postal.**
I would like to send a telegram to...	**Quisiera mandar un telegrama a...**

COMPLAINTS. Tourism is Spain's leading industry and the government takes complaints from tourists very seriously.

C The majority of disputes in hotels and restaurants are due to misunderstandings and linguistic difficulties and should not be exaggerated. As your host wants to keep both his reputation and his licence, you'll usually find him amenable to reason. In the event of a serious problem, you can demand a complaint form *(Libro Oficial de Reclamaciones)*, which all hotels and restaurants are required by law to have available. The original of this triplicate document should be sent to the regional office of the Ministry of Tourism; one copy stays with the establishment against which the complaint is registered and you keep the third.

Recent legislation greatly strengthens the consumer's hand. Public information offices are being set up, checks carried out, and fallacious information made punishable by law. For a tourist's needs, however, the tourist office, or, in really serious cases, the police, would normally be able to handle it or, at least, to advise you where to go.

CONSULATES *(consulado).* Almost all Western European countries have consulates in Barcelona. All embassies are located in Madrid.

Australia. Gran Vía Carlos III 98, 9th floor; tel. 330 9496

Canada. Via Augusta, 125; tel. 209 06 34

Eire. Gran Via Carles de III, 94, l0th floor; tel. 330 96 52

South Africa. Gran Via de les Corts Catálanes, 634; tel. 301 55 83

U.K.* Avinguda Diagonal, 477; tel. 419 90 44

U.S.A. Via Laietana, 33; tel. 319 95 50

---

* Also for citizens of Commonwealth countries

CRIME and THEFT. The Barcelona Urban Security Council gives this advice: don't leave your luggage unattended; don't carry around more money than you'll need for daily expenses; use the hotel safe deposit for larger sums and valuables; in crowds around street attractions and sports events, be on your guard against pickpockets; reject offers of flowers or other objects from street pedlars—they may be after your purse; wear cameras strapped crosswise on the body; don't leave video cameras, radio cassettes and valuables in view inside your car, even when locked; photocopy personal documents and leave the originals in your hotel.

Once nominated the Olympic site, Barcelona began clearing the city centre streets of drug pushers, pickpockets and other petty crooks preying on tourists. The blue-clad mobile regional anti-crime squads are out in force on the Rambla and principal thoroughfares, with visible results. Should you be the victim of any theft or crime, report it at once to the nearest police station *(comisaría)* and to your consulate. Each year, more *comisarías* are staffed with interpreters. During the summer months interpreters are posted at

Via Laietana 49, tel. 302-6325, and at Carrer Ample 23, tel. 318-3689.

I want to report a theft.	**Quiero denunciar un robo.**
My handbag/ticket/wallet/	**Me han robado el bolso/**
passport has been stolen.	**el billete/la cartera/el pasa-**
	porte.

DRIVING. Crossing the border into Spain, you won't be asked for documents, but in the event of any problem you will have to produce a valid driver's licence, proper registration papers and a "Green Card" extension of your regular car insurance to make it valid in foreign countries. This can be obtained from your insurance company or at the border. An International Driving Permit has the advantage of a translation in Spanish, but is not required of most Europeans or Americans. Check with your automobile club for the latest information before your departure.

With your certificate of insurance, you are strongly recommended to carry a bail bond. If you injure someone in an accident in Spain, you can be imprisoned while the accident is being investigated. This bond will bail you out. Apply to your home automobile association or insurance company.

Your car should display a nationality sticker near the rear licence plate. Seat belts are not compulsory within the city limits, but not using them on the motorway is punishable by a fine. Most fines are payable on the spot.

Parking. Don't take any chances parking "just for a minute" in a no parking area. You may come back to find a yellow triangular sticker affixed to the spot, with instructions (in Catalan) on how to find your towed-away car. A heavy fine will await you.

In any event, there are many underground parking facilities and garages marked with a big blue and white "P" in the centre of the city, as well as clearly marked (in blue) sections of the side streets that parallel the main boulevards, with ticket vending machines (coin or credit-card operated) for up to two hours' parking (nights and Sundays excepted). Tickets have to be placed on the dashboard, visible from outside.

Speed limits. Maximum speed is 120 kph (75 mph) on motorways, 100 kph (62 mph) or 90 kph (56 mph) on other roads, 60 kph (36 mph) in towns and built-up areas. Cars towing caravans (trailers) are restricted to 80 kph (50 mph) on the open road.

D **Fuel**. Petrol stations are marked on city maps, but they may not carry a full range of super, normal and diesel, so fill up when you see what you require. There are a few pumps providing unleaded fuel in the city. A coin or two tip for the attendant is customary.

Fluid measures

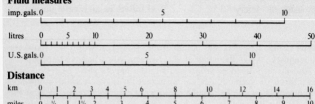

Distance

Road signs. Most road signs are given in both Spanish and Catalan, accompanied by the standard symbols used throughout Europe.

(International) Driving Licence	**Carnet de conducir (internacional)**
Car registration papers	**Permiso de circulación**
Green card	**Carta verde**
Are we on the right road for...?	**¿Es ésta la carretera hacia...?**
Full tank, please.	**Llene el depósito, por favor.**
normal	**normal**
super	**super**
lead free	**sin plomo**
Please check the oil/tyres/ battery.	**Por favor, controle el aceite/ los neumáticos/la batería.**
Can I park here?	**¿Puedo aparcar aquí?**
My car has broken down.	**Mi coche se ha estropeado.**
There's been an accident.	**Ha habido un accidente.**

DRUGS. Once notorious for wide-open drug dealing in the Plaça Reial area, Barcelona now is cracking down on pedlars. Drugs are strictly illegal.

E **ELECTRIC CURRENT** *(corriente eléctrica)*. 220 volts is standard, but some hotels have a voltage of 110–120 in bathrooms as a safety precaution. Check before plugging in any appliance.

Sockets (outlets) take round, two-pin plugs, so you will probably need an international adaptor plug, on sale at hardware stores and airports. Visitors from North America will need a transformer unless they have dual-voltage travel appliances.

What's the voltage?	**¿Que voltaje es?**
an adaptor/a battery	**un transformador/una pila**

EMERGENCIES. (See also CONSULATES, MEDICAL CARE, POLICE, CRIME.) The National Police emergency number (in and outside Barcelona) is 091; dial 092 for the traffic police and 080 in the event of fire.

Careful!	**Cuidado**	Police!	**Policía**
Fire!	**Fuego**	Stop!	**Deténgase**
Help!	**Socorro**	Stop thief!	**Al ladrón**

ENTRY and CUSTOMS FORMALITIES *(aduana)*. Nationals of Great Britain, Eire, the U.S. and Canada need only a valid passport to visit Spain, and even this requirement is waived for the British, who may enter on a visitor's passport. A national identity card is sufficient for citizens of most Western European countries. Visas are required for some Latin American and African countries, as well as for Australia and New Zealand: check with your travel agent if in doubt. Persons coming from yellow fever or cholera zones may be required to produce an immunization card.

The following chart shows customs allowances for certain items of personal use.

Into:	Cigarettes		Cigars		Tobacco	Spirits		Wine
Spain 1)	300	or	75	or	400 g.	1.5 l.	and	5 l.
2)	200	or	50	or	250 g.	1 l.	and	2 l.
Australia	200	or	250 g. or		250 g.	1 l.	or	1 l.
Canada	200	and	50	and	900 g.	1.1 l.	or	1.1 l.
Eire	200	or	50	or	250 g.	1 l.	and	2 l.
N. Zealand	200	or	50	or	250 g.	1.1 l.	and	4.5 l.
S. Africa	400	and	50	and	250 g.	1 l.	and	2 l.
U.K.	200	or	50	or	250 g.	1 l.	and	2 l.
U.S.A.	200	and	100	and	3)	1 l.	or	1 l.

1) Visitors arriving from EEC countries.
2) Visitors arriving from other countries.
3) A reasonable quantity.

E **Currency Restrictions**: Visitors may bring as much Spanish or foreign currency as they wish into the country without a declaration. Departing, though, the limit is 100,000 pesetas and the equivalent of 500,000 pesetas in foreign currency. If you intend to bring in and take out again larger sums, declare this on arrival and departure.

G **GUIDES** *(guía)*. Licensed guides may be engaged through the Associ-ació Professional de Guies Turístics de Barcelona; tel. 345-4221. Hotels and travel agencies will also put you in touch with qualified guides and interpreters.

We'd like an English-speaking guide.	**Queremos un guía que hable inglés.**
I need an English interpreter.	**Necesito un intérprete de inglés.**

H **HAIRDRESSERS** *(peluquería)* and **BARBERS** *(barbería)*. Luxury hotels have their own salons and the others can direct you to a reputable establishment. Prices vary widely.

HEALTH and MEDICAL CARE. There are seven public first-aid sta-tions *(Centros de Asistencia Primaria)* in different districts of Barcelona, open from 8 a.m. to 2 p.m. (from 9 a.m. on Sundays and holidays), and an emergency service at Carrer de Numància 23 (tel. 230-7000), open from 5 p.m. to 9 a.m. during the week and around the clock on Sundays and holidays. Emergencies requiring surgery are handled at the Centro Quirúrgico de Urgencia on the Avinguda de les Drassanes, behind the medieval shipyard (tel. 241-0600). The Hospital de la Santa Creu i de Sant Pau has an emergency coronary unit (tel. 348-1049) and outpatient clinics covering most ailments. The better hotels have arrangements with a doctor on call or can direct you to one of the private clinics.

A special Spanish health and accident insurance for tourists (ASTES) covering doctor's fees and clinical care may be obtained through your travel agent at home or in Spain. Visitors from EEC countries with corresponding health-insurance facilities are entitled to medical and hospital treatment under the Spanish social security system. Before leaving home, ensure that you are eligible and have the appropriate forms.

Pharmacies *(farmacia)* operate during normal business hours but there is always one in every district that is open all night and on holidays. The location and phone number of this *farmacia de guardia* is posted on the door of all the other *farmacias*.

Contraception. With the growing problem of AIDS *(SIDA)*, strong Roman Catholic opposition has been overcome and contraceptives are easily available from pharmacies, public toilets and other less likely places. The word for a condom is *preservativo*.

Where's the nearest (all-night) pharmacy?	**¿Donde está la farmacia (de guardia) más cercana?**
I need a doctor/dentist.	**Necesito un médico/dentista.**

HOURS. Barcelonans are not as addicted to the siesta as other Spaniards. The big department stores, some main bank branches and shops remain open all day and factories also work full shifts. Other than this, very few shops open all day, usual hours are from 9.30 a.m. to 1.30 p.m. and 4.30 to 8 p.m. Monday to Saturday. Government offices and the vast majority of businesses are open from 9 a.m. to 2 p.m. and from 4 p.m. to 7 p.m. or later. Restaurants start serving lunch around 1 p.m. until 3 p.m. and dinner from between 8–9 p.m. until 11 p.m. or later.

LANGUAGE. Both Catalan and Castilian Spanish are official languages in Catalonia, and virtually all the people a traveller encounters will speak Spanish, even though regional government policy and the personal preference of native Barcelonans favour Catalan. Street signs are all in Catalan, museum labels and menus usually in both languages. The European-minded Barcelonans frequently speak French, English or Italian. Nevertheless, learning and using some courtesy phrases in Catalan will earn you a smile of appreciation. Here are a few:

ENGLISH	CATALAN	CASTILIAN
Good morning	**Bon dia**	*Buenos días*
Good afternoon	**Bona tarda**	*Buenas tardes*
Good night	**Bona nit**	*Buenas noches*
Thank you	**Gràcies**	*Gracias*
You're welcome	**De res**	*De nada*
Please	**Si us plau**	*Por favor*
Goodbye	**Adéu**	*Adiós*

The Berlitz phrase book SPANISH FOR TRAVELLERS covers most situations you are likely to encounter during your stay in Barcelona. The Berlitz Spanish-English/English-Spanish pocket dictionary contains 12,500 concepts, plus a menu-reader supplement.

Do you speak English?	**¿Habla usted inglés?**
I don't speak Spanish.	**No hablo español.**

L **LAUNDRY** *(lavandería)* **and DRY-CLEANING** *(tintorería)*. Most hotels will do laundry the same day and dry-cleaning overnight, but they'll usually charge more than a laundry or a dry-cleaners.

Where's the nearest laundry/dry-cleaners?	**¿Dónde está la lavandería/ tintorería más cercana?**
When will it be ready?	**¿Cuándo estará listo?**
I must have this for tomorrow morning.	**Lo necesito para mañana por la mañana.**

LOST PROPERTY. The police office for *objetos perdidos* has the phone number 301-3923. To report a lost credit card, phone American Express (217-0070), Eurocard (302-1428), Master Charge or Visa (315-2512).

I've lost my wallet/handbag/ passport.	**He perdido mi cartera/bolso/ pasaporte.**

M **MAPS and STREET NAMES**. Since 1985, all street names in Barcelona and most Catalan towns have been posted in Catalan. Towns have reverted to their Catalan names, too. Lérida is Lleida, San Carlos is Sant Carles, etc. Maps before this time may still have names in Spanish and even quite different names. Some words that crop up frequently:

CATALAN	CASTILIAN	ENGLISH
Avinguda	*Avenida*	Avenue
Carrer	*Calle*	Street
Església	*Iglesia*	Church
Palau	*Palacio*	Palace
Passeig	*Paseo*	Boulevard
Passatge	*Pasaje*	Passageway
Plaça	*Plaza*	Square

Many Barcelona streets are one way and/or do not permit turns to left or right. The give-away tourist maps do not have streets catalogued and keyed to the map. Buy a good street map and save time and trouble. The *Guía Urbana de Barcelona* handbook is most comprehensive and contains much useful information. The maps in this book were prepared by Falk-Verlag, Hamburg, who also publish a detailed map of Barcelona.

I'd like a street plan of...	**Quisiera un plano de la ciudad de...**
a road map of this region	**un mapa de carreteras de esta comarca**

116

MEETING PEOPLE. The people of Barcelona are genuinely friendly, proud of their city and do not look contemptuously on people who speak their language badly. They'll go out of their way to give you directions. If you are male, it isn't difficult to start up conversations with your neighbour in a snack bar or bus by commenting on the fortunes of the Barça football team. Movies, pop music cassettes and current concerts are opening gambits with young people.

Good manners dictate that when addressing anyone about anything at all, in person or on the telephone, you begin by saying *bon dia* or *buenos días,* followed by *senyor, senyora* or *senyoreta,* as appropriate. A handshake on greeting and leaving is normal.

MONEY MATTERS

Currency. The monetary unit of Spain is the *peseta* (abbreviated pta.).
  Banknotes: 1,000, 2,000, 5,000, 10,000 pesetas.
  Coins: 1, 5, 10, 25, 50, 100, 200 and 500 pesetas.
  A 5-peseta coin is called a *duro* and prices are sometimes quoted in duros, e.g., 10 duros = 50 ptas.

Banking hours are traditionally from 8.30 a.m. to 2 p.m., Monday through Friday, till 1 p.m. on Saturdays (except June through August). More and more banks now keep their central offices downtown open until 5 p.m. There is no rule on this, so take note of the times posted on the bank doors. Private money changers and travel agencies with a *cambio* sign will serve you outside banking hours. There are money-changing facilities in the Sants and Término-França railway stations open from 8 a.m. to 8 p.m. (10 p.m. in summer). On Sundays, the Sants station office is closed between 2–4 p.m. The airport exchange counter is open every day from 7 a.m. to 11 p.m. (10 p.m. in summer, when it is also closed on Sundays). Banks do not always keep the rates posted near the door up to date. You may not receive what you expected. Traveller's cheques get a bit more than cash. Take your passport with you when changing money. Hotels and shops charge a considerable mark-up when changing money.

Credit cards. Internationally recognized cards are accepted by hotels, restaurants and businesses in Spain. You can even use some to pay tolls on the motorway if you reach the frontier without having changed money. But best check in advance which ones are accepted before relying on yours.

Eurocheques. Most hotels and department stores take Eurocheques. **117**

M

Where's the nearest bank/ currency exchange office?	**¿Dónde está el banco/la oficina de cambio más cercana?**
I want to change some pounds/ dollars.	**Quiero cambiar libras/ dólares.**
Do you accept traveller's cheques?	**¿Aceptan cheques de viaje?**
Can I pay with this credit card?	**¿Puedo pagar con esta tarjeta de crédito?**

N NEWSPAPERS and MAGAZINES *(periódico; revista)*. The many newsstands and bookstalls along the Rambla carry the day's leading English, German and French newspapers and *The International Herald Tribune*. A good selection of European and American magazines is also available.

Have you any English-language newspapers/magazines?	**¿Tienen periódicos/revistas en inglés?**

P PHOTOGRAPHY. Many shops in midtown will develop and print colour film in an hour or two. All popular brands of film are on sale. Customs regulations limit importing film to 10 rolls per camera.

Airport baggage scanners won't hurt your film, exposed or not.

A haze filter is a good investment and will protect your lens. Remember that noonday shots will have a bluish tone, while early morning and evening pictures overemphasize red.

I'd like a film for this camera.	**Quisiera un carrete para esta máquina.**
How long will it take to develop (and print) this film?	**¿Cuánto tardarán en revelar (y sacar copias de) este carrete?**

POLICE. There are three police forces: the *Policía Municipal* on traffic duty with white-and-blue-checked hat bands, the blue-uniformed *Policía Nacional,* an anti-crime brigade that usually patrols in pairs or is motorized, and the *Guardia Civil,* a national force assigned to rural areas and recognizable by their patent leather hats (now being phased out). Interpreters are stationed at a few central police stations *(comisarías)*. See also CRIME AND THEFT.

Where's the nearest police station?	**¿Dónde está la comisaría más cercana?**

PUBLIC HOLIDAYS *(fiesta)*. Certain public holidays change from year to year. The local government publishes a list of holidays at the beginning of each year.

January 1	*Año Nuevo*	New Year's Day
January 6	*Epifanía*	Epiphany
May 1	*Día del Trabajo*	Labour Day
June 24	*San Juan*	St. John's Day
August 15	*Asunción*	Assumption
September 11	*Fiesta Nacional de Catalunya*	Catalonia National Day
September 24	*Día de la Mercè*	Day of Our Lady of Mercy
October 12	*Día de la Hispanidad*	Discovery of America (Columbus Day)
November 1	*Todos los Santos*	All Saints' Day
December 6	*Día de la Constitución Española*	Constitution Day
December 25	*Navidad*	Christmas Day
December 26	*San Esteban*	St. Stephan's Day
Movable Dates:	*Viernes Santo*	Good Friday
	Lunes de Pascua	Easter Monday
	Lunes de Pentecostés	Pentecost
	Inmaculada Concepción	Immaculate Conception (normally December 8)

In addition there are special festivities in the different *barris* (districts) of Barcelona during the year, especially in late August.

RADIO and TELEVISION *(radio; televisión)*. National broadcasting on the two state-run channels is in Spanish, with one local station in Catalan. The better hotels have one or more satellite channels providing programmes in English, French and German. Voice of America and the BBC are received clearly on short wave.

RELIGIOUS SERVICES *(servicio religioso)*. Roman Catholic mass is said regularly in the churches of Barcelona, great and small. The French Parish at Carrer d'Anglí 15 has an English-language service the first and third Sundays of the month at 10.30 a.m. The Anglican church of St. George at Sant Joan de la Salle holds Sunday services at 11 a.m. The

R Greek Orthodox church is located at Carrer d'Aragó 181, the Jewish community synagogue is at Carrer de l'Avenir 24, and the al-Widadiyah mosque is at Carrer de Balmes 13.

T **TIME DIFFERENCES**. Spanish time coincides with that of most of Western Europe—Greenwich Mean Time plus one hour. In spring, clocks are put forward an hour for Daylight Saving Time (Summer Time).

Summer Time chart:

New York	London	**Spain**	Jo'burg	Sydney	Auckland
6 a.m.	11 a.m.	**noon**	noon	8 p.m.	10 p.m.

What time is it?   **¿Qué hora es?**

TIPPING. Service is almost always included in hotel and restaurant bills, though not always indicated. If in doubt, ask "¿Está incluido el servicio?" A further tip of a few coins is appropriate, as is a little something for porters, bellboys, etc. Follow the chart below for rough guidelines.

Airport or station porter	100 ptas. per bag
Hotel porter, per bag	200 ptas.
Maid, for extra services	100–200 ptas.
Waiter	5% (optional)
Taxi driver	5%
Tourist guide	10%
Hairdresser	10%
Lavatory attendant	25–50 ptas.
Usher	25–50 ptas.

TOILETS. There are many expressions for "toilets" in Spanish: *aseos,* **120** *servicios, W.C.* and *retretes*. The first two are the most common. Toilet doors are distinguished by a "C" for *"Caballeros"* (gentlemen) or "S" for *"Señoras"* (ladies) or by a variety of pictographs.

In addition to the well-marked public toilets in the main squares and stations, a number of neat coin-operated toilets in portable cabins marked *W.C.* are installed at convenient locations around the city. Just about every bar and restaurant has a toilet available for public use. It is considered polite to buy a coffee or glass of wine if you drop in specifically to use the conveniences.

Where are the toilets?   **¿Dónde están los servicios?**

TOURIST INFORMATION OFFICES *(oficinas de turismo)*. Spain maintains tourist offices in many countries. These offices will supply you with a wide range of colourful and informative brochures and maps in English. If you visit one, you can consult a copy of the master directory of hotels in Spain, listing all facilities and prices.

Australia. International House, Suite 44, 104 Bathurst St., P.O. Box A-675, 2000 Sydney NSW; tel. (02)264 79 66

Canada. 102 Bloor St. West, 14th floor, Toronto, Ont., M5W 1M8; tel. (416) 961 31 31

United Kingdom. 57–58 St. James's St., London SW1A 1LD; tel. (071) 499 1169

United States. Water Tower Place, Suite 915 East, 845 North Michigan Ave., Chicago IL, 60611; tel. (312) 944-0216/230-9025

1221 Brickell Avenue, 33131 Miami, Florida; tel. (305) 358 1992

8383 Wilshire Blvd., Suite 960, 90211 Beverly Hills, CA 90211; tel. (213) 658-7188/93

665 5th Ave., New York, NY 10022; tel. (212) 759-8822

Barcelona. At the Barcelona airport, railway stations and on the Moll de la Fusta, on the quay at the foot of the Rambla, information and hotel reservation desks with multilingual staff can help you get oriented and provide a programme of events for the month. The city's tourist authority, the Patronato Municipal de Turismo, is at

Passeig de Gràcia 35, 08007 Barcelona; tel. 215 44 77.

The Ajuntament (City Hall) citizen's information phone number around the clock is 010. There are also electronic bulletin boards at strategic **121**

T locations that list sporting and cultural events and other information continuously.

Where is the tourist office?   **¿Dónde está la oficina de turismo?**

TRANSPORT. Barcelona has an excellent network of buses, metro lines, funiculars, a suburban railway and a lovely old blue tram, a relic that goes part way up Mt. Tibidabo. In the Plaça de Catalunya, a point where many lines start or converge, you can buy combination ten-ride tickets good on all facilities (except for train stops outside the city, such as the airport) and at the same time pick up a free map of these services. Using this ticket on the automatic machines at the front of the buses and at metro turnstiles saves time. The same ticket can be used for your whole family—just have it punched once for each person up to ten times. During the summer, one-, three- and five-day tickets for unlimited rides are also available. You can, of course, buy (more expensive) single tickets from the bus driver or from metro, funicular or tram ticket booths. Ten-ride tickets can only be bought in the Plaça de Catalunya, at metro stations or in the following "Caixes" (savings banks): Caixa de Pensions, Caixa de Catalunya and Caixa de Barcelona.

A very good bet from June 24 to September 15 is the "Barcelona Singular" combination ticket covering all services and the bus No. 100. This bus leaves the Pla del Palau every 45 minutes and follows a special touristic route all over the city. In 90 minutes it covers most of the places you'll want to visit, and you can hop on and off as often as you wish.

Metro. Barcelona's underground railway crosses the city more rapidly than other forms of transport and runs from 5 a.m. to 11 p.m. weekdays and to 1 a.m. Saturday. On Sundays and holidays service is from 6 a.m. to 1 a.m. The station entrances are marked with a red diamond outlining the word "metro".

Buses. Bus stops are covered and list the numbers and routes of the buses on that route, including the hours of service. Most buses run from 6.30 a.m. to 10 p.m., but on the main routes some run all night long. If you're waiting for a bus after 10 p.m., better check the timetable.

Taxis are black with yellow trim and there are lots on the streets at all hours. A green light and/or a *libre* (vacant) sign shows when the cab is empty. Taxis bear the initials SP *(servicio público)* on front and rear bumpers.

Ferries connect Barcelona to Palma de Mallorca daily and serve Menorca and Ibiza six times a week in summer. There is a weekend cruise

operated by the Compañía Transmediterránea to Palma, stopping at
Ibiza, using the ship as a hotel for two nights.

Trains. Spain's national railway, the RENFE *(Red Nacional de Ferro-
carriles Españoles)* operates fast and punctual long-distance trains
throughout the Peninsula and to international connecting points. Seat
reservations are essential during holidays and the summer season. Tickets may be bought in travel agencies as well as in the central Sants station
from where international trains depart. They all stop for passengers
in midtown at the Passeig de Gràcia underground station, useful for
travellers with a hotel in the Eixample district. The Estació de França in
the harbour area is being remodelled and is scheduled to reopen as
Barcelona's main terminal in late 1990. This is also the station used for
local trains going up the coast.

The Generalitat de Catalunya (regional government) operates local
trains to the suburbs, including points of interest to tourists. These run on
the same tracks as metro lines. The train to Montserrat and Manresa
leaves from the Plaça d'Espanya. The Plaça de Catalunya station serves
the Autonomous University of Barcelona, Sant Cugat and Terrassa.

RENFE honours Inter-Rail, Rail-Europ and Eurail cards (the latter
sold only outside Europe), and offers other discounts to youths (under 26)
and seniors (over 65). Many discounts reach 50 per cent. Anyone
intending to use the train to reach Barcelona or to travel outside it will do
well to find out about current discount tickets from a travel agency, local
railway station or, in Barcelona, from the information desk in the central
station or by phoning RENFE (322-4142). Certain lines will carry your
car at a discount, too.

When's the next bus/train to...?	**¿Cuándo sale el próximo autobús/tren para...?**
A ticket to...	**Un billete para...**
single (one-way)	**ida**
return (round-trip)	**ida y vuelta**
What's the fare to...?	**¿Cuánto es la tarifa a ...?**
first/second class	**primera/segunda clase**

WATER. Barcelona's water is safe, but it is so heavily chlorinated as to
be almost unpalatable. Good bottled water is available, fizzy *(con gas)* or
flat *(sin gas)*, and some shops even sell this water in plastic bubbles to
make unchlorinated ice cubes.

a bottle of mineral water	**una botella de agua mineral**
Is this drinking water?	**¿El agua es potable?**

WEIGHTS AND MEASURES. Spain uses the metric system.

Temperature

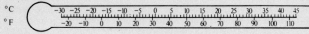

Length

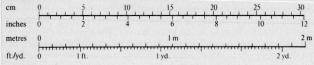

Weight

grams	0	100	200	300	400	500	600	700	800	900	1 kg
ounces	0	4	8	12	1 lb	20	24	28	2 lb.		

DAYS OF THE WEEK

Sunday	**domingo**	Thursday	**jueves**
Monday	**lunes**	Friday	**viernes**
Tuesday	**martes**	Saturday	**sábado**
Wednesday	**miércoles**		

NUMBERS

0	**cero**	11	**once**	30	**treinta**
1	**uno**	12	**doce**	40	**cuarenta**
2	**dos**	13	**trece**	50	**cincuenta**
3	**tres**	14	**catorce**	60	**sesenta**
4	**cuatro**	15	**quince**	70	**setenta**
5	**cinco**	16	**dieciséis**	80	**ochenta**
6	**seis**	17	**diecisiete**	90	**noventa**
7	**siete**	18	**dieciocho**	100	**cien**
8	**ocho**	19	**diecinueve**	101	**ciento uno**
9	**nueve**	20	**veinte**	500	**quinientos**
10	**diez**	21	**veintiuno**	1,000	**mil**

SOME USEFUL EXPRESSIONS

yes/no	**sí/no**
please/thank you	**por favor/gracias**
excuse me/you're welcome	**perdone/de nada**
where/when/how	**dónde/cuándo/cómo**
how long/how far	**cuánto tiempo/a qué distancia**
yesterday/today/tomorrow	**ayer/hoy/mañana**
day/week/month/year	**día/semana/mes/año**
left/right	**izquierda/derecha**
up/down	**arriba/abajo**
good/bad	**bueno/malo**
big/small	**grande/pequeño**
cheap/expensive	**barato/caro**
hot/cold	**caliente/frío**
old/new	**viejo/nuevo**
open/closed	**abierto/cerrado**
here/there	**aquí/allí**
free(vacant)/occupied	**libre/ocupado**
early/late	**temprano/tarde**
easy/difficult	**fácil/difícil**
Does anyone here speak English?	**¿Hay alguien aquí que hable inglés?**
What does this mean?	**¿Qué quiere decir esto?**
I don't understand.	**No comprendo.**
Please write it down.	**Escríbamelo, por favor.**
Is there an admission charge?	**¿Se debe pagar la entrada?**
Waiter!/Waitress!	**¡Camarero!/¡Camarera!**
I'd like...	**Quisiera...**
How much is that?	**¿Cuánto es?**
Have you something less expensive?	**¿Tiene algo más barato?**
Just a minute.	**Un momento.**
Help me, please.	**Ayúdeme, por favor.**
Get a doctor, quickly!	**¡Llamen a un médico, rápidamente!**

Index

An asterisk (*) next to a page number indicates a map reference. Where there is more than one set of page references, the one in bold type refers to the main entry.

039/208 SUD